INNER YOGA

Yogacharya Dharmananda
(Swamiji)

This book was printed in the United States of America, and published by Meadows Photography, Inc..

To order additional copies of this book, please contact:
sdharmananda@yahoo.co.in
inneryoga1@gmail.com

Beloved Krishna
Be Thou O! Krishna the charioteer of my life
And help me to free myself from this mortal strife

BELOVED KRISHNA

Beloved Krishna my heart so genuinely longs
To make my life Your creative song;
I wish to bloom in such a way
That Your beauty gets reflected the purest way.

This desire to reflect You in me
Is what I carry deep within me;
Will You Krishna, will You help me
Please do, please do I implore Thee.

You have given me much of what I wanted
You have given me so much even unwanted;
Will You now do me this last big favor
Help me to reflect Your beautiful flavor.

MY WORSHIPFUL SHIKSHA GURU LINEAGE

Beloved masters, please accept my heartfelt prostrations at Your blessed feet. Countless blessings have flowed in my life since I received your sacred teachings. Please guide my footsteps steadily towards the eternal Light.

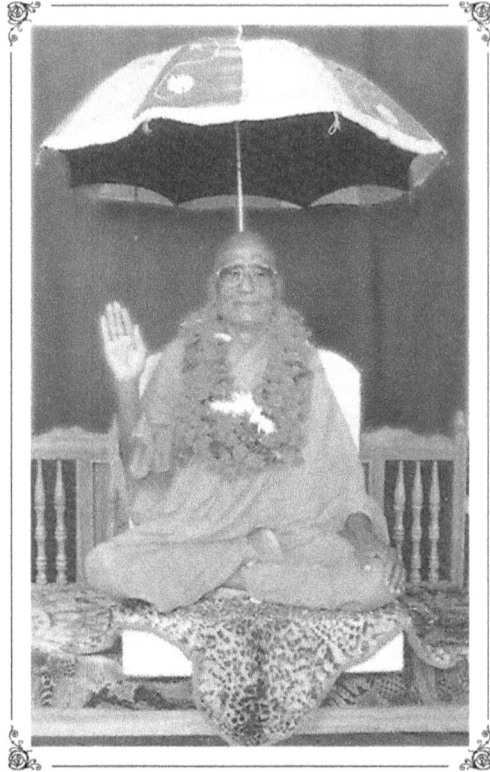

H.H. Shri Vishwaguruji Maharaj, Mahamandaleshwar

Founder-President

International Vishwaguru Meditation and Yoga Institute
Ved Niketan Dham, Swargashram
Rishikesh, Uttaranchal (Himalaya), India

MY DIKSHA GURU

Om Shri Vishvaguruve Namah

To
H.H. Yogsamrat Vishwaguruji Maharaj, Mahamandaleshwar

I lived and studied at the Ved Niketan Dham Swargashram for twenty-five years. It was a lovely place, set in the foothills of the mighty Himalayas, over looking our Mother Ganga— ever-flowing and redeeming.

In all those years, my respect and admiration for Shri Mahamandaleshwar continued to grow. With single minded purpose and utmost devotion, he worked for more than forty years to build the ashram and the Yoga Institute. To this day, I continue to marvel at his many gifts:

The strength to endure extremes of heat or cold and the ability to live without food for long periods of time,

The tenacity to withstand constant criticism, and his total control over speech and emotion,

The strength to remain calm and self possessed in stressful or provocative situations, or when destiny took a bad turn,

His sharp memory and remarkable ability to quote the scriptures,

His unfailing determination, persuasive skill, and executive ability.

His willingness to overlook mistakes, even at the risk of creating difficulties for himself.

Rejecting no one, embracing all, he is the measure of everything I hope achieve.

Mata Santosh Bharti (Mataji)

D/o Late Bhai Kishan Chand and Late Vidya Devi of
Marada, Punjab

Spiritual Successor of H.H. Shri Vishwaguruji Maharaj

International Vishwaguru Yoga Meditation Institute
Ved Niketan Dham, Swargashram, India

I wish to express my deep gratitude for the role you played
in my inner transformation. You absorbed all my anger,
irritability, harsh speech, and repeated wrong behavior, and
never ever reacted harshly.

You were always very understanding, accepting, and forgiving. Your thirty-five years of unconditional personal service to Late Vishwaguruji Maharaj, your freedom from all ambitions and desires, and your deep state of abiding inner peace was a glowing example for me to imitate. I can never in anyway return the love and service you gave me for the past twenty-five years. I will always remain deeply indebted to you in every way.

To Bhartiji with Gratitude

Dear Bhartiji on this b'day (13.4.03)
My heart is longing something to say;
In my life the role you played
Brought me much peace in words cannot be said.

Many a conflicting desire and need
In my life I had to face;
As I struggled with my inner pain
Your presence was my only solace.

Always comforting, always kind
Never reacting, never unkind;
For all future guidance upon you I look
With a grateful heart to you, I dedicate this book.

Valerie Meadows

To Swamiji

THE ONE

In deep prayer and longing,
I fall to my knees
Realizing I am but a servant
To the divine

I am but an offering
To the greater realms
Invisible to many
Visible to the One

I am in awe of how vast
And yet so intimate
This Eternal Being is with me
To caress without touching
To kiss with only my heart

A passionate union
With only my soul

My body useless
But so important
In bringing together
The Love from everywhere

To be shared
A participant to something far beyond
Any understanding
Consuming, intoxicating, expanding

A birth into a new life
With love as my guide
A better servant
Filled only with the One

And me diminishing
No longer needed
Only the One . . .
Only the One. . .

JOINING WITH THE FOREVER

Floating for a moment in a sea of eternal bliss
Small lights flying around
Each waiting for an opening
To penetrate into my heart and soul.

My heart - with its long journey in this life
Covered with a veil of uncertainty and longing

Waiting, always for the gentle sweetness
Of the Divine love to cleanse me
To a state of uncompromising purity
Such a necessary preparation for the final journey.

Lifting beyond the need to return to the cycles of
    birth and rebirth
For test and instruction . . . such relief.
My soul - a formless presence vibrating always
From the deepest part of me and extending into infinity
Profound knowledge, illumined colors, energy everywhere.

Limitless, boundless, waiting with patience and such
    urgency
Waiting for an opening from my shell
The shell, created from limitation, ignorance
Weakness and blindness "to the joining."

The shell, part of what this life defines as "me"
Obliterate me, to unite with the Forever.
I am nothing, I am everything
I am moving towards my final breath
To be at last, completely full.

V. M.

DEDICATION

Shri Lal Mohan Das

Dear father,

As you live the last part of your life, I wish to convey my heart's deepest feelings to you.

I remember every bit of my childhood, when you took so many pains to see that I had the best education in English and modern science. You sacrificed a brilliant professional career in the railways, and vacated a grand ancestral property in Varanasi, to take care of my needs at home in Kolkata. You did not marry a second time in deference to my special needs and fears. You waited until I became an adult and graduated from a prestigious Military Academy with a Gold medal to my credit; you sacrificed your career and your happiness for my sake.

As you live the last days of your life, please know that the prophecy, which was made in the majestic Himalayas to my Grandfather, that a child will be born to you who will bring credit to the family and the country, is now coming true. Though I had my doubts, you always believed in me.

You lived an austere life, sacrificed all your personal needs and happiness to save enough for my education in English and Science. You enrolled me in a military school, where I was groomed for a brilliant career as an officer in the Indian Armed Forces, and where I also learned the values and discipline necessary to form the basis for a strong spiritual foundation.

Please know that the work your own father had entrusted in you has been realized through me in America, where I am teaching.

May the best health, happiness, and deep satisfaction be upon you at all times.

ACKNOWLEDGEMENT

I would like to thank Julia Jacobs for her devotional service, having spent so much of her time and creative energy converting my manuscript into book form.

I would also like to thank Mata Santosh Bhartiji (Mataji) for her unfailing encouragement to complete this work.

Lastly, I would like to thank Valerie Meadows for her photographs, and for her unfailing faith and devotion to this project.

To my Guru, Paramahansa Yoganandaji, whose teachings have given me the greatest soul satisfaction.

To Shri Vishwaguruji Maharaj, for giving protection to me and providing me with the environment and training for my spiritual growth.

Table of Contents

1 INNER STRUGGLE

2 SELF ENQUIRY

3 MY HEART FELT PRAYERS

4 INSTRUCTIONS FROM GOD/GURU OR THE SOUL WITHIN

5 MY EXPERIENCES

6 MY INNER STRUGGLE RESOLVED

7 APPRECIATION TO STUDENTS AND FRIENDS

8 STUDENT'S EXPRESSING GRATITUDE

9 INDIA SHINING

MY INNER STRUGGLE AND UNFOLDING PEACE BLISS AND LOVE

1

INTRODUCTION

I was distinctly uncomfortable with myself in my early twenties. I suffered great pain and didn't know why; I couldn't explain it, let alone find a remedy for it. I strived to do the right thing, but my thoughts and feelings were often wrong and negative.

This inner struggle was so intense and persistent that I was eventually forced to give up a brilliant military career.

I began to practice Yoga and meditation in my early thirties in an attempt to find peace with myself. As my practice deepened, I began to get an understanding of these difficulties. I also found remedies.

These insights, expressed as poetry in this book, were divinely inspired and served as a source of inner guidance for me. I am hopeful that these sentiments may also provide similar inspiration to a troubled soul.

CONSCIOUS AND SUBCONSCIOUS MIND

My conscious and subconscious mind
Their thoughts and tendencies are opposite in kind;
This creates inside a tension very strong
Resulting in actions and behavior wrong.

Consciously I always like to unite
Subconsciously I tend to divide;
Consciously I like the idea of serving
Subconsciously there is no such feeling.

Consciously I wish to be warm and bold
Subconsciously I know there is fear and am cold;
Consciously I know am educated and wise
Subconsciously however this is not so I realize.

Consciously I wish to freely mix
Subconsciously I withdraw and selectively mix;
Consciously I wish to be out and active
Subconsciously I am in and inactive.

Consciously I wish to be calm and polite
Subconsciously I am often angry and impolite;
Consciously I like to respect authority
Subconsciously I know I dislike authority.

Consciously I take care to be honest and truthful
Subconsciously I am not always so careful;
My knowledge often theoretical
I fail to apply correctly in affairs practical.

This creates in me much pain
Everything around me is beautiful, yet inside only pain.

31-7-2000
Sarnath

2

STRUGGLE IN MY MIND

My conscious and sub-conscious mind
Is involved in a struggle peculiar in kind;
Creates in me a personality trait
That is divisive making me often fume and fret.

With all my education and training
I have not been successful in resolving;
I find myself – a personality split
And in many ways a social misfit.

31-7-2000
Sarnath

MY DIVIDED CONSCIOUSNESS

My inner problem is clear as day light
But what do I do to resolve it, is not in sight;
My consciousness is fractured and split
What do I do to integrate it?

Yoga I know is a science of oneness
Resolves and integrates all aspects of consciousness;
Yet I am unable to make the necessary change
Everything seems confusing and really very strange.

My Guru's teachings I know is full of light
But practicing the techniques I found no delight;
My mind always looked for teachings here and there
But never found satisfaction going anywhere;

Consciously I feel my Guru's teaching is beautiful
Subconsciously however I am often very resentful.
What do I do? Oh, what do I do?
To resolve this difficulty what do I do?

31-7-2000
Sarnath

MY SOUL AND MY MIND

My soul and my mind
Opposed to each other in kind;
Creates a tension strong
And often actions wrong.

My soul longs to create
And flood my being with joy;
My mind it's tamasic state
Crushes this desire to enjoy.

Love all equally
My soul so declares;
My mind says stubbornly
Him, not him who cares.

My soul hungers constantly
To work for social gain;
My mind's frustrating incapacity
Turns this hunger into pain.

31-7-2000
Sarnath

2

SELF ENQUIRY

This intense inner struggle to understand myself forced me to give up a brilliant army career and family life. I left for Rishikesh when I was thirty in search of spiritual teachings.

MY MIND ENQUIRING

My soul you are infinite
Infinite and free;
Why do you remain
Tied to this tree?

Why don't you break
And make yourself free;
Why do you remain
Tied to this tree?

My soul you are omnipotent
All power is in you;
With what power then
My mind binds you?

Why don't you break
And make yourself free;
Why do you remain
Tied to this tree?

My soul you are light
All light is in you;
How then my mind
Creates darkness around you?

Why don't you break
And make yourself free;
Why do you remain
Tied to this tree?

My soul you are joy
All joy is in you;
How then my mind
Creates unhappiness around you?

Why don't you break
And make yourself free;
Why do you remain
Tied to this tree?

31.7.2000
Sarnath

MY MIND ENQUIRING

Eastern sky, full-moon rising
Western sky, evening star shining
My mind quietly brooding
Body gently pacing.

Why am I here
What am I doing?
From here when I leave
Where will I be going?

I wish to recollect the memory of the past
And look into the future with a vision vast;
I do not want any cultural belief parroting
I seek a truthful, honest knowing.

Who am I
Why am I here?
Will You tell me my Lord
And make this clear.

03.05.04
Ved Niketan, Swargashram

SOURCE OF ANGER

Anger, anger where is your source
From where do you get so much force?
You spring so suddenly
Overpowering me completely.

What makes you from nowhere rise
Taking me so totally by surprise;
I never consciously call for you
You come when I least need you.

Anger, anger know for sure;
Your evil consequences I will calmly endure.
I will, however, not allow you this freedom;
To ruin my peace and destroy my wisdom.

18-8-2000
Ved Niketan, Swargashram

LIFE IS STRANGE

Life is strange events are strange
Circumstances are all so very strange;
What is their purpose often I have enquired
No answers came I felt so tired.

My heart remained sad and life was joyless
Everything around me felt so meaningless;
But as I sat quietly and looked within me
The circumstances and their purposes got revealed to me.

I am slowly learning that life is very dear
Everything that happens brings a message quite clear.

31-8-2000
Ved Niketan, Swargashram

I WISH TO KNOW

Life is strange how much do we know
So much pain and suffering why do we undergo?
Why what for our hearts do cry
Never a satisfying answer, however, hard we try.

I wish to know, I wish to know
Why this painful experience I wish to know;
What actions of mine created the cause
I wish to know the broken laws.

Even if you are told what will you gain?
You still have to bear this present pain;
Do not waste your time dwelling on the cause
Use the present moment practicing Divine laws.

11-10-2000 --
Ved Niketan, Swargashram

3

MY HEART FELT PRAYERS

KRISHNA PLEASE COME

Krishna Krishna when will You come
Just for once please do come;
Come come Krishna come
My heart longs for Thee please do come.

Oh Krishna, how many times I have called You
How many nights I have cried for You;
You never came, even for once
I never saw You, even by chance.

If You do not come, how can I purify
The faults of my mind, so difficult to rectify;
This dirt this ego in me
Only You O Krishna can help me

It is in Thy light – darkness flies away
It is in Thy presence – faults fall away.

20-8-2000
Ved Niketan, Swargashram

MY LORD MAKE ME WHOLE

Open up, open up
Brain centers, open up;
Open up, open up
Crown chakra, open up.

Rise up, rise up
Kundalini rise up;
Rise up, rise up
To the crown rise up.

Flow down, flow down
Divine energy flow down;
Flow down, flow down
Divine consciousness flow down.

Make whole, make whole
My vision, make whole;
Make whole, make whole
My being, make whole.

3-8-2000
Sarnath

MY LOVE

My Love, my Love
Come to me;
My Love, my Love
Heart belongs to Thee.

My Love, my Love
No more hide;
My Love, my Love
Heart open wide.

My Love, my Love
Make me full;
My Love, my Love
Full-ly full.

3-8-2000
Sarnath

MAKE ME YOU

Make me warm
And full of charm;
Make me smiling
And joy permeating.

 Make me loving
And motherly caring;
Make me good
For good's sake good.

Make me You
Small but You;
Make me You
Oh Lord! Make me You.

3-8-2000
Sarnath

KRISHNA SHED YOUR LIGHT

Krishna, Krishna in darkness I sleep
Day and night I weep and weep;
Krishna, Krishna where is Your Light?
Please bring Your Light, oh bring Your Light.

Light, Light Your Light I crave
Long have I been my ego's slave;
Pain and tension I have created enough
Bound by these chains I have lived enough.

Freedom, freedom, this I seek
I feel so weak, so very weak;
No strength have I for self-effort
Your presence is now my only comfort.

Will You come, will You come
Tell me Krishna when will You come?
Weak and low I lie in bed
Waiting for a little light to be shed.

Decide Krishna, what will You do
Wait and hope, nothing else can I do;
This battle between ego and Self is a hard one
Only through Your grace this battle is won.

21-8-2000
Ved Niketan, Swargashram

KRISHNA KILL MY EGO

Krishna come, Krishna come
On this birthday, please do come;
Come, come and kill my ego
Let it go, oh! let it go.

Enough, enough I had enough
This damn annoying ego-stuff;
Away with it, oh! away with it
Krishna dear, kill it kill it.

23-8-2000
Ved Niketan, Swargashram

KRISHNA COME TO ME

Will You dear Krishna for once come to me
 If not for anything else just to reassure me;
You have in the past so graciously did appear
To so many of Your devotees am I not Your dear?

Will You not for once give me the pleasure
To see Your divine form for my eyes to treasure.

Speak to me my Lord bold and clear
Make me obey You by force or by fear;
Punish me my Lord every time I stray
Never allow it, humbly I pray.

14-3-2001
Dharamshala

KRISHNA FILL MY MIND

Fill my mind, fill my mind
My beloved Krishna fill my mind;
With thoughts of Thee, thoughts of Thee
In deep devotional longing for Thee.

My mind is generally blank this is not good
With no ideas and plans it often falls into mood;
You have given me a life with very little responsibility
But how do I make use of it with no inner creativity?

My dear Krishna please do something
How can I be happy doing practically nothing?
My mental state badly needs a change
Only through Your grace I know I can change;

So beloved Krishna it is up to You
Do as You wish I surrender to You.

15-3-2001
Dharamshala

I SURRENDER TO YOU

With a heart full of anguish I implore Thee
Shower upon me Oh! shower upon me;
Thy power Thy love and let me know Thy will
I wish to work, but only in tune with Thy will.

All personal desires and all personal cravings
I renounce at Thy feet and seek only blessings;
My life in Your hands it is up to You
Do as You wish I surrender unto You.

15-3-2001
Dharamshala

EGO YET TO GO

My mind is blank I have learnt its okay
I will not feel bad and let it be that way;
This vacant mind as a begging-bowl in hand
At Your door-step I will indefinitely stand.

I realize any impatience that I may tend to show
Is that much of my ego yet to go;
Yes impatience is a very big thorn
I have to remove it before I am reborn.

15-3-2001
Dharamshala

HELP ME TO OVERCOME HARSH SPEECH

Please give me control over my conscious speech
Sub-consciously also I do not desire harsh speech;
Make me simple, humble, and polite in every way
I wish to practice this with each passing day.

Krishna why my speech is often harsh
I desire to be soft yet invariably I am harsh;
Why this lack of control I feel so bad
Help me overcome this I feel very sad.

2-4-2001
Dharamshala

KRISHNA PLEASE COME

Krishna, Krishna when will You come
Krishna, Krishna please do come;
Come, come Krishna come
Long have I waited please do come.

This anguish in my heart
When will this end;
When will You come
Tell me dear Friend.

Even though You promised
My Guru did not come;
I will keep on waiting
For him and You to come.

My Guru will come
And You will also come;
I will keep on waiting
For You and him to come.

Please come soon
Oh! Please come soon;
I am tired of waiting
Please come soon.

10-5-2002
Ved Niketan, Swargashram

KRISHNA I SEEK ONLY YOU

Krishna Krishna where are You
Krishna Krishna I love only You;
Krishna Krishna no more hide
Krishna Krishna my heart open wide.

I wait for You, I wait for You
I love to see and experience You;
Krishna Krishna are You coming
How long will you keep me waiting?

You have surrounded me with so much human love
I however crave for Your Divine love;
Be so kind and come to me
I seek only Thee, only Thee.

2-5-2002
Ved Niketan, Swargashram

MY LORD PLEASE COME

Deep in my heart
I am very sure;
I am as yet
Not so pure.

But I will wait
And patiently pray;
For You my Lord
To come and stay.

My heart in pain
Yearns for Thee;
When will You come
When shall I see.

My Lord, my Lord
Please do come;
Deep in my heart
 Your Name I hum.

I know I am lazy
And negligent may be;
But can You my Lord
Deny my longing for Thee.

My longing is genuine
Sincere and strong;
Come my Lord and let my
Heart sing Your song.

My heart is in pain
But it knows very well;
You will surely come
Just when will You please tell.

The longing in my heart
Intensifying each day;
I shall keep on waiting
Please come when You may.

23.8.02
Ved Niketan, Swargashram

COME MY LORD AND BRING MY GURU

When will You my Lord
Bring joy to my heart?
This nagging hollow feeling
When will this depart?

When will I see
Your blessed Divine form;
When will I feel
Your joy in this human form?

When will You my Lord
Guide me to my Guru?
When will my training
Begin with my Guru?

Am I not qualified
To begin my training?
How do I purify
Without the training?

Come my Lord
And bring my Guru;
I deeply long
For him and You.

10.10.02
Ved Niketan, Swargashram

KRISHNA PLEASE REVEAL YOUR SELF

I wish to tune my mind
In such a loving way;
Never by arrogance, ignorance or mistake
From Your wish to stray.

The love in my heart
Is a product of weakness;
I however wish
I love you for your goodness.

The mind always craves
For money and worldly fame;
It is so difficult to make it understand
The richness of Your Name.

Reveal to me my Lord
The sweetness of Your glories;
How long do I continue
Hearing them in stories.

20.03.03
Ved Niketan, Swargashram

DISSOLVE ME IN YOU

My Lord, it is You
Who have become me;
Will You now please
Within You dissolve me.

I no longer wish to identify
With this body or mind;
To do as You wish
I leave them behind.

This body's pain and laziness
They are from now Yours;
The mind's dullness and weaknesses
Are also all Yours.

In any form of karma or dharma
I no longer wish to involve;
I remain detached with this hope
Within You to dissolve.

5.12.03
Ved Niketan, Swargashram

WHEN WILL THE BLESSED DAY COME

When will the day come my Lord
When my eyes will have the power;
To see Your glory shining
In every face or flower.

When will the day come my Lord
When through every word or action;
I can reflect your love and joy
And receive in return sweet satisfaction.

When will I my Lord get up each morning
With Your name on my lip;
When will that nectar of immortality
My mind shall be able to sip.

Help me, help me my Lord
To reach that blessed state;
Free me, free me my Lord
From this present unsatisfying state.

15.5.03
Ved Niketan, Swargashram

SEND ME A GURU

Blossom forth, blossom forth
I wish to blossom forth;
In love, beauty and song
Is this desire wrong?

Why then this waiting so long
My Lord! Is this desire wrong?
Send me a Guru, send me a Guru
Please dear Krishna send me a Guru.

To open my heart
And let my love flow;
And in the light of creativity
Let all my actions glow.

Tell me dear Krishna
Is this desire wrong?
To express Your joy and beauty
Is this desire wrong?

Why do You then
Make me wait so long?
What have I done
So wrong, so wrong?

5.11.2001
Ved Niketan, Swargashram

OPEN MY EYES TO SEE THE LIGHT

Day by day and night after night
Sing and dance till you see the Light;
He is near and everywhere
My eyes are closed I see Him nowhere.

Open my eyes, open my eyes
My heart in anguish deeply cries;
Respond my Lord with Your healing touch
And quench this thirst that I feel so much.

4.4.05
Ved Niketan, Swargashram

MY GURU COME

My Guru, my Guru
Please do come;
Help me, help me
Let me overcome.

With your loving grace
Lit a smile on my face;
Ignite the fire of wisdom
And let me roam in freedom.

Free me from my pain
And my karmic chain;
Let me my peace regain
Let me in bliss remain.

11-05-2002
Ved Niketan, Swargashram

TO LORD RAMA

Your B'day is being celebrated
In every temple and many a home;
Locked in my room pacing and circling
With a heart heavy I roam.

To worship You in Your temple
I have no desire;
To worship Your symbol at home
I have again no desire.

But yes my Lord
I do have a desire;
In love and devotion to Thee
I wish to set my heart afire.

I wish to live my life
In such a way;
That Your wisdom and qualities
Get reflected in every way.

But being unable to do so
I live so much in pain;
Accepting myself the way I am
No peace comes –it appears vain.

Accept yourself, accept yourself
I am flooded with this advise;
My heart never responds to it
No joy or strength arise.

What is the answer my Lord
To this difficulty I face;
Am I creating this situation
Let me know the truth showering Thy grace.

12.4.03
Ved Niketan, Swargashram

4

INSTRUCTIONS FROM GOD/GURU
OR
THE SOUL WITHIN

MY SOUL SPEAKS TO MY MIND

The voice within says hello dear
Do you hear, do you hear?
Stop your senseless cravings
All your restless desirings.

Stop all your seeking
All thy ceaseless running;
Be quiet, sit still and look within
You will find everything, just go in.

The mind replies yes dear
I hear, I hear;
I am quiet and am in
I am still and looking within;

But who are You and where are You?
I see myself but not You.

My activities were restless in the external
Similar do I see them in the internal;
I was same there
As I see myself here;
But who are You and where are You?
I see myself but not You.

The voice within says hello dear
Come, come, I am here, I am here;
Just behind your thoughts I am there
Just behind those emotions I am there;
Come, come, I am hear, I am hear
Come, come, I am near, very near.

I see my thoughts, they are clear
I see my emotions, restless as ever;
But behind them where are You
I see You not, where are You?
I am here, I am here
I am here, near and everywhere.

Are you joking, are you fooling
I am looking and looking;
You say, You are here, near, everywhere
But I do not see You anywhere;
Everything I want You said, I will find looking within
But emptiness, darkness and void that's all I see in.

I am going, I am going
This is not what I am seeking;
Do not go, stay a while
In this emptiness, rest a while.

Oh no! What's happening? What's happening?
I am dying, I am dying;
No, no – you are waking, you are waking
Ah ha!! I was dreaming, I was dreaming;
Peace, joy, love all that I was craving
I am myself That, what I was seeking.

31.7. 2000
Sarnath

DIRTY LAYERS IN THE MIND

Please observe dear mind
By deeply going in;
And you will surely find?
The dirty layers therein;
Layer upon layer, dirt of every kind
This is your accumulation oh my dear mind.

You always cry
Seeking Divine help;
But do you really try
A little self-help.

Did you not know the faults that you see
Are a mere reflection of what is in thee;
Did you ever care to rectify your self
Before you wanted others to rectify themselves.

So my dear mind
Do not look behind;
Do not regret, do not resent
But move on in the present;
Acknowledging the dirt is in itself washing
Repent and regret, that will do the flushing.

But do not despair
Keep up your cheer;
You will soon find
Oh my dear mind;
The peace that you are seeking
The joy that you are craving.

1.7. 2000
Sarnath

EGO IS THE PROBLEM

Ego, ego that's the problem
What you think is not the problem;
Offshoots, offshoots they are of ego blocks
Crush this ego, everything will unlock.

Bow down, bow down
Everywhere bow down;
Bow down, bow down
To everything bow down.

Bow down, bow down
Do not judge;
Bow down, bow down
Keep no grudge.

Bow down, bow down
That's the way;
Bow down, bow down
Ego to slay.

16-8-2000
Sarnath

EGO CREATES MISERY

Watch every action
Every little re-action;
See the ego play
Creating misery everyday.

Everything you express
With a desire to impress;
Every little exhibition
With a desire for appreciation;

Is a vain ego play
Creating misery everyday.

28-7-2000
Sarnath

HELPING OTHERS IS EGO PLAY

I want to help, I want to help, this is your ego
Give up this idea let it completely go;
I want to give, I want to give, what can you give
Steeped in ignorance what will you give?
Wake up, wake up, wake yourself up
Then will you know how to wake others up.

31-8-2000
Ved Niketan, Swargashram

SEEK MY LIGHT NOT LIMELIGHT

Limelight, limelight
You seek limelight?
My Light, My Light
What about My Light?

Give me this, give me that
You always cry give me, give me;
Stop all crying for this or that
Cry if you wish only for Me.

Me, Me only Me
Day and night seek only Me;
Nothing, nothing, only Me
Remember, remember, only Me.

As you seek Me be very clear
I will take away all that is dear;
If you cling to things that are dear
Know for sure I will never be near.

31.7. 2000
Sarnath

DO NOT REACT STRONGLY

Do not react so strongly
On actions done wrongly;
Your judgment of wrong and right
May not be so bright.

31.7. 2000
Sarnath

SOFTEN YOUR SPEECH

Your speech is very taunting
Harsh and often rude
Your indirect boasting
Reflects nature crude.

Soften, soften down my mind
Make your nature loving and kind;
Let all your actions be gentle and caring
Your mannerism smiling and loving.

31.7. 2000
Sarnath

STOP MY MIND

Stop, stop my mind
The least exaggeration of every kind;
All tall talk, all wrong talk
All hurting and hitting talk;

All dramatizing and emotional talk
All in-direct self-glorifying talk;
Stop, stop my mind
All loose talk of every kind.

31.7. 2000
Sarnath

BE SIMPLE

Be simple, be simple my mind
It is so easy to be nice and kind;
Why do you unnecessarily frown?
And turn your table up-side down;
Think, think, what do you gain?
Pain, pain only pain.

31.7. 2000
Sarnath

DO NOT CRITICIZE

Do not criticize, do not criticize
Those who habitually tell lies;
They are slaves of their lying habit
Why do you have to strongly hit?
Turning them from friend to foe
And creating for yourself misery and woe.

31.7. 2000
Sarnath

STOP SAYING I CANNOT DO

Stop this unholy parroting
I cannot do, I cannot do;
What you think you cannot do
Is the very thing you have to do.

This is how the striving soul
Marches on towards it's goal;
By saying I cannot, you take a step backward
By asserting I can, you move a step forward.

With each step forward, joy is what you gain
With each step backward, what you get is pain;
So choose well between gain and pain
What you choose you will surely gain.

31.7. 2000
Sarnath

BE HAPPY

Be happy
In whatever you do;
Be happy
In whatever you do not do.

Be happy
In whatever you can do;
Be happy
In whatever you cannot do.

Be happy
In whatever you want to do;
Be happy
In whatever you do not want to do.

Be happy
In joy and in gain
In sickness and in pain;
In happiness
And in unhappiness
Be happy.

31.7. 2000
Sarnath

CHANT DIVINE NAME

Divine Name, Divine Name
Divine Name is nectar;
Divine Name, Divine Name
There is nothing more sweeter?

Divine Name, Divine Name
This is your mantra;
Divine Name, Divine Name
Keep chanting this mantra.

Divine Name, Divine Name
Repeat this mantra;
Divine Name, Divine Name
Be engrossed in this mantra.

Divine Name, Divine Name
Visualize this mantra;
Divine Name, Divine Name
Perfect this mantra.

Divine Name, Divine Name
Loose yourself in this mantra;
Divine Name, Divine Name
Become one with this mantra.

Divine Name, Divine Name
This is what you master;
Divine Name, Divine Name
There lies all the answer.

3-8-2000
Sarnath

BREAK HABIT PATTERNS

My conscious mind your efforts do strengthen
The sub-conscious patterns needs to be broken;
The job is hard needs determined fight
But do not give up – that's not right.

The conscious and sub-conscious their conflicting state
Do get resolved in the super-conscious state;
Pray and chant and deeply meditate
To reach as quickly that blessed state.

3-8-2000
Sarnath

PURIFY YOUR HEART

Purify your heart, purify your heart
That's what is required to master spiritual art;
No studies, no lecturing, no glamour required
A heart truly purified if that is acquired.

Purify your heart, purify your heart
What is more fulfilling than this Divine art;
Honor, positions, titles, name and fame
These are nothing, sweeter Divine Name.

Sweeter Divine Name, Sweeter Divine Name
Chant my mind, holy Divine Name;
Holy Divine Name, holy Divine Name
Chant my mind, holy Divine Name.

31-8-2000
Ved Niketan, Swargashram

CHANGE YOURSELF

Wrong, wrong you are wrong
Your speech and mannerism they are wrong;
Change, change yourself change
Who are you to make others change?

Let everybody be as they are
Who are you to make changes there?
Learn to be one with good and bad
Make no judgments and give up being sad.

Who are you do you know this
Who are they have you thought of this?
You and they are one in Me
Why are you then fighting with Me?

Stop all judgments be at peace
Stop all criticism be a peace;
Smile at everybody be at peace
Bow down everywhere be at peace.

Change, change my dear
It is you who need to change be very clear;
What do you think why are you here
To change only yourself, you are here.

31-8-2000
Ved Niketan, Swargashram

MEDITATE

Meditate, meditate
Whole day meditate;
Meditate, meditate
As much possible meditate.

Meditate, meditate
It will surely reveal;
Meditate, meditate
The causes of your weal.

Meditate, meditate
All answers will come;
Meditate, meditate
And problems over come.

16-8-2000
Sarnath

LIFE IS A PLAY

Open my heart, bloom, bloom
Why do you cry gloom, gloom?
Why do you feel doom, doom
Open my heart, bloom, bloom.

Do you not feel the joy around you
Do you not see Nature smiling at you?
Do you not hear the voice within you
Saying, life is a play between Me and you.

Do you not see in the boxer's ring
How much torture do they bring?
Yet the boxer's return to the ring
Willingly enduring so much hurting.

That is how life's pain must be borne
Loss and defeat also should be known;
Are passing phases in this game
Live your life, for His sake, in His name.

3-8-2000
Sarnath

RETURN TO THY GLORY

Sun is rising
Birds are chirping;
Flowers are blooming
You are sleeping.

Enough of this dreaming
Enough of this sleeping;
Finish with this misery
Return to thy glory.

3-8-2000
Sarnath

SUPPRESSED EMOTIONS

Subconsciously activated angry reaction
Is frequently creating a lot of tension;
In all my personal relation
Helpless I feel am seeking a solution.

Do you remember Guruj's instruction
Sit longer in meditation;
That is your only solution
So practice more meditation.

As you sit a little bit longer
And make this practice a bit more stronger;
From deep within your sub-conscious mind
Suppressed emotions of many a kind;
Like air bubbles in water will rise up
Slowly one by one they will come up.

As they rise you will become aware
Sit and watch do not react, beware!
If you react they will again go down
And your sincere effort will simply drown.

Rising up to the conscious level, they will get released
Deep within you, you will feel very pleased;
This process of rising and releasing
And the mind bit by bit emptying;
May go on for weeks, months or a year
Till the whole stock is completely clear.

How big your stock, only Sadguru's know well
And I am sure they will never fore-tell;
So persevere my mind and never give up
When you are free, your life will cheer up.

22-8-2000
Ved Niketan, Swargashram

SEEK DIVINE TREASURES

From deep within comes wisdom and power
Pouring profusely like thunder and shower;
The pleasures outside they promise much
Fulfilling them gives no satisfaction as such.

No more crave, no more crave
This craving in the past produced misery very grave;
Forego my mind all these pleasures
Go deep within and seek Divine treasures.

23-8-2000
Ved Niketan, Swargashram

JEALOUSY

Seeing your neighbor progress never feel bad
Do not become jealous do not go mad;
If your neighbor progresses offer him your hand
Both of you will progress hand-in-hand.

This is Divine wisdom blessed and pure
Your neighbor 's success will be yours know for sure;
If on the other you work to pull him down
He may or may not but you will surely drown.

Jealousy this jealousy my mind
Give rise to pains of many a kind.

31-8-2000
Ved Niketan, Swargashram

MAKE THE EFFORT

Make the effort make the effort
My mind make the effort;
How many years have you been in pain
How many more years you want the pain?

Make the effort make the effort
My mind make the effort;
Do not give up do not give up
Every little effort will help you rise up.

Sit my mind a bit more sit
There's no other way do it do it;
Day by day and night after night
Keep up your practice till you see the light.

31-8-2000
Ved Niketan, Swargashram

NEVER STOP TRYING

Light is there love is there
Joy is there power is there;
Everything is there everything is there
Deep within you everything is there.

Within, within that is the secret
Going in never will you regret;
Try my mind keep on trying
Success or failure never stop trying.

31-8-2000
Ved Niketan, Swargashram

GIVE UP IDENTIFICATION

Give up all identification
With family, state or nation;
Rise above caste, creed or religion
Break the barriers creating division.

Anger, hatred, jealousy, residing in our heart
Destroys all good will and breaks peace apart;
O my dear mind, learn this lesson well
Transform these emotions and get rid of the hell.

If you do not do this, your chakra-kundalini awakening
Is a vain ego effort which will never be freeing.

31-8-2000
Ved Niketan, Swargashram

LET'S GO HOME

Come dear mind let's go home
Long have you wandered no more roam;
No more roam, no more roam
Come dear mind let's go home.

Let's go back to our joyous plane
What are you seeking in this lower plane?
All the pleasures here in this sense plane
Are mere shadows of the Divine Plane.

Remember that state, remember that state
Whence have you come to this lower state;
Let's go back, let's go back
To that Divine state, let's go back.

31-8-2000
Ved Niketan, Swargashram

LEARN TO LIKE WHAT YOU DIS-LIKE

Why are you here, why are you here
Again and again remind yourself, why are you here?
You are here to learn to like
That which your heart so much dislike.

Do you not know that Raga and Dwesha
Creates much klesha; Patanjali said so Centuries ago.

Then do you now realize
What makes a person wise?
He is wise who has learnt to like
That which his heart so much dislike.

8-9-2000
Ved Niketan, Swargashram

DO NOT FIGHT OTHERS FAULTS

Observe everything do not react
Strange are human ways this is a fact;
Your needs my needs never are same
When there's a difference why do you blame?

Life is graded no one is perfect
We have all our own defects;
When you see a fault out there
Why do you fight that – is it fair?

Others have more faults, you have less
But you also are not fully fault-less;
Why do you fight then why do you fight
What do you gain and is this action right?

8-9-2000
Ved Niketan, Swargashram

SHOW RESPECT

Respect, respect everybody respect
Respect even those who dis-respect;
Do not hurt them those who hurt you
Love them even more, those who hate you.

This is Divine life at it's best
Practice, practice pass each test;
As you practice this Divine art
Peace and bliss will fill your heart.

8-9-2000
Ved Niketan, Swargashram

EMPTY THE MIND

Reading, reading
Stop all reading;
Emptying, emptying
Begin emptying.

Reading fills the mind from outside
But is never fully satisfying;
Emptying fills the mind from inside
And is supremely satisfying.

Ramakrishna, Ravindranath, Einstein, Mozart
Never had any schooling in science or art;
Yet what profound wisdom came in spate
From their blissful inner state.

22-8-2000
Ved Niketan, Swargashram

PRACTICE SILENCE

Silence, silence this is your need
In this thought take heed, take heed;
Stop all activities they cannot bring
The joy of the soul, in silence do spring.

23-8-2000
Ved Niketan, Swargashram

PRACTICE WHAT YOU PREACH

You always say I do not speak
I, however, know I speak and speak;
You do not listen, what do I do?
You do not obey, what can I do?

Obey, obey learn to obey
Right or wrong you just obey;
It is I who speak make no judgment
Through every face they are My instrument.

You always claim you love Me
But do you really care to listen to Me;
If you do not listen then what is this love
And what do I do with this sort of love?

You have to practice what you have taught
Never try to pretend what you are not;
Do first yourself what you teach
Put into practice what you preach.

8-9-2000
Ved Niketan, Swargashram

BE TRUTHFUL

Be truthful be truthful
My mind be truthful;
In every little thought
Whether it is pleasing or not.

In every little action
And every little reaction;
Be truthful be truthful
My mind be truthful.

Every little thought and action
Will attract towards you a similar reaction;
So be watchful of how you pass your day
And ever so careful with what you do and say.

10-10-2000
Ved Niketan, Swargashram

REMOVE THEM

Remove them remove them
Painstakingly remove them;
What do you mean
What should I remove?

Your angry words and sentiments
Your quick emotional judgments;
Your uncontrolled pronouncements
Your ideas of personal accomplishments.

Because your Krishna taught
And maybe you forgot;
God is equally present in the killer and the killed
In the sinner and the sinned.

So whom can we blame
And why should we blame?

11-10-2000
Ved Niketan, Swargashram

LOVE ALL

Love all love all my mind love all
Open out your heart to all to all;
Allow this emotion of love to flow freely
Do not block its path through judgments silly;
If you do so what do you gain
A block within gives only pain.

11-10-2000
Ved Niketan, Swargashram

THE DIRTIEST DIRT

Do not react do not react;
In praise or in blame
Remain ever the same
Practice, practice this act.

Why do you say do not blame me
What do you loose when other 's blame thee?
What is that which feels the hurt
It is your ego the dirtiest dirt.

11-10-2000
Ved Niketan, Swargashram

SOCIAL WORK

Social work, social work
This desire for social work;
Is great and appears very impressive
But do you really care to find out its motive?

Glorification, my dear glorification
That's the only motivation;
So give up this desire
And to a secluded spot retire.

Spend your days well practicing each day
Intensifying Divine longing, day by day.

11-10-2000
Ved Niketan, Swargashram

FILL THE MOMENTS WITH THOUGHT OF GOD

Fill the moments of leisure
In the thought of God;
Enjoy the moments of pleasure
In gratefulness to God.

All your depressions all your sadness
All your frustrations all your weakness;
They are Maya's tool
Making you a fool.

My mind know this for sure
Not to get affected is the only cure;
Apply this lesson well
Never allow them in you to dwell.

11-10-2000
Ved Niketan, Swargashram

DROP YOUR WANTS

Drop your wants all your needs
They are products of karmic seeds;
In wisdom fire roast these seeds
In the present do not create more needs.

These desires my mind always lead to pain
Even when satisfied gives no permanent gain;
To fulfill these desires you so much always crave
Life is short time is running soon you'll be in grave.

On so many occasions you saw yourself
Satisfying these desires do not really help;
Every time you fulfill a desire the mind asks for more
The demand never ceases give me more.

Desires are mirages they do not give joy
Stop my mind playing with this toy;
Go deep within and realize you are
Already full and perfect having infinite power.

23-1-2001
Ved Niketan, Swargashram

DESIRES NEVER SATISFY

Ego wants to revel in appreciation and praise
From its realm my mind raise yourself raise;
Long, long my mind only for Krishna
Reject like poison every other trishna.

You are always craving for fame and money
That's precisely what sages call poisoned honey;
Give up, give up my mind this desire is vain
Never will it satisfy, will create only pain.

23-1-2001
Ved Niketan, Swargashram

IDENTIFICATION

Identification with the body
The wise say is bad;
They always keep you moody
Unhappy and sad.

Identification with the mind
Can be twice as bad;
It creates such a hell
And makes you go mad.

Long have I been
Suffering in this hell;
I am now determined
No more here will I dwell.

Freedom from identification
Is a boon indeed;
It makes you feel so light
And that's what we need.

Thanks to you beloved Christine
Your joy and love pristine;
Brought me this message loud and clear
My heart is in love, joy and cheer.

13-3-2001
Dharamshala

MY MIND AWAKEN

Awaken, awaken
My mind awaken;
To thine own potential
Do thou fully awaken.

You are not
What you always feel;
You are Divine
Heal yourself heal.

Express, express
Do not shrink;
All those beautiful thoughts
You always think.

Thoughts are real
Be careful as you deal;
Use them rightly
To heal yourself heal.

What you think
You will create that;
What you feel
You will become that.

So rightly think
And rightly feel;
That is how my mind
Heal yourself heal.

14-3-2001
Dharamshala

CHANGE YOUR FEELINGS

Observe dear
Observe your feelings;
They are wrong
Change these feelings.

Feel your love flowing
And your joy bubbling;
Feel your heart expanding
And your mind awakening;
Feel you are creative
And very very active.

Our feelings determine
What we are;
Know their importance
Understand their power.

Thoughts and feelings
Two important tools;
Keep them positive
This is Divine rule.

19-3-2001
Dharamshala

SEEK DIVINE WITHIN

Leave my mind leave
The sensory door;
Move on dear move on
To the Divine shore.

The desires within you
There is no end;
How long will you wander
Tell me dear friend.

My mind turn
Turn deep within;
Give up all desiring
Seek the Divine within.

Do what you want
You will never feel satisfied;
Unless you go within
And have your desires fried.

26-3-2001
Dharamshala

LIFE IS SWEET

Beautiful, beautiful
Everything is beautiful;
Cheerful, cheerful
Be always cheerful.

Never think bad
Never feel sad;
Never get mad
Enough you have had.

Life is sweet
Everything is sweet;
Please make the effort
To be more and more sweet.

27-3-2001
Dharamshala

LEARN TO GO MORE IN

My mind work, work hard
And develop your receptivity;
Practice, practice more sincerely
And increase your sensitivity.

A little better concentration
Will lead to inner inspiration;
But there is this need my mind
To deepen your meditation.

The creativity that you aspire
The energy that you desire;
They are there but deep within
You have to learn to go more in.

28-3-2001
Dharamshala

THE EYE-BROW CENTER

Concentrate my mind concentrate
On the eye-brow center;
Withdraw yourself inward
And hold on to this center.

Stop your scattering
And all your chattering
Gaze hard and long
Be determined and strong.

The darkness in-front
Will slowly give way;
To a joyous light
Revealing the cosmic highway.

28-3-2001
Dharamshala

LIFE IS FULL, BE BRAVE

I am full
I am full;
Life is full
Everything is full.

Full of love
Full of joy;
Full of peace
I en-joy.

Nothing I am lacking
Nothing I am missing;
This is my own
Wrong inner feeling.

It is easy to be happy
When life is kind;
Brave hearts remain happy
When it is unkind.

Let me not despair
While carrying own cross;
Let me remember the brave ones
Who have carried other 's cross.

**29-3-2001
Dharamshala**

LEARN TO SMILE

Smile my dear smile
Look into the mirror;
And learn to smile
Smile my dear smile.

Smile a loving smile
Smile a warm smile;
Smile a knowing smile
Smile an affectionate smile

Smile an understanding smile
Smile a friendly smile.
When you look at somebody smile
When you are tired smile;

When you are annoyed smile
When you are sad smile;
When you are alone smile
Smile at all times smile.

Many ailments will get cured as you smile
Tensions and fatigue get released with a smile;
Hard feelings and enmity ceases with a smile
All boredom vanishes with a smile.

Light up your face with a smile
Bring more energy in the body with a smile;
Do everything in your life with a smile
Let God reflect in you in your smile.

30-3-2001
Dharamshala

PRACTICE CONCENTRATION

Restless, restless
My mind you are restless;
Be still, be still
Be a bit more still.

Close your eyes
Thoughts will rise;
Let them come and let them go
Do not check or control their flow.

Observe carefully the mental space
Varying colored lights will come and go;
You will see yellowish, bluish or whitish glow
Let your consciousness in this light flow.

Concentrate my mind concentrate
More deeply concentrate;
For higher experiences
This light you have to penetrate.

30-3-2001
Dharamshala

THE WORLD CAN NEVER SATISFY

O my Krishna, O my Krishna
Come, please come dear Krishna
It is You, it is You
Through all my seeking, I seek only You.

I realize this clearly
Deep in my heart;
Every time I seek something
It keeps me and You apart.

My mind is sure of this
The world can never satisfy;
Yet the absence of a taste of bliss
The world I try to justify.

Give me a taste
O Lord give me a taste;
Enough have I wandered
Come please make haste.

My mind is always divided
Between the world and You;
Sometimes it seeks the world
At other times it turns towards You.

31-3-2001
Dharamshala

LEARN TO BEHAVE

My mind please behave
Please do behave;
Follow religiously the instructions
Your Guru gave.

Be gentle, soft and polite
In interactions with all;
Drop all likes and dislikes
Mix freely equally with all.

Be soft, be soft
In the smallest of your actions;
Keep a check, keep a check
In every little reactions.

2-4-2001
Dharamshala

APPRECIATE WHAT YOU HAVE

Grace is there
Help is there;
Blessings are there
Everything is there.

Peace is there
 Joy is there;
Strength is there
Everything is there.

Become aware, become aware
My mind become aware.

Be thankful
Be grateful;
Be joyful
Be cheerful.

You always cry
For what you do not have;
Why don't you try
Appreciating what you so much have.

30-5-2001
Almora

EXERT MORE

How long, how long
My mind how long?
Will you remain a slave
In spite of the teachings your Guru gave;
How long will you continue in life
Grief-stricken, weak with inner strife.

Wake up, wake up
Exert your will;
As you do so
Your life will slowly fill.

With strength and creativity
Keen receptivity;
Varied ability
Utmost enjoyability.

So exert, exert
Do not divert;
Let the energies flow inward
Slowly take them upward.

There at the top of your brain
As you learn to remain;
You will experience cosmic light
Bestowing peace and ever-new delight.

7-6-2001
Almora

JUST BE WHAT YOU ARE

Drop all impatience
Drop all frustrations;
Just be what you are
Just be what you are.

There is no need for projection
There is no need to create impression;
Just be what you are
Just be what you are.

Stop this fighting with yourself
Stop this struggle with yourself;
Stop being sad with yourself
Stop further hurting yourself;
Just be what you are
Just be what you are.

You do not have to become something
You do not have to achieve something;
Just be what you are
Just be what you are.

Accept yourself as you are
Love yourself as you are;
Just be what you are
Just be what you are.

11-6-2001
Almora

BE CALM

My mind, be calm
Very calm, very very calm.

Let nothing create a disturbance within you
Let nothing be able to provoke you;
Let there be no struggle within you
Let there be no demands within you.

Each day practice more meditation
This will reduce all the inner agitation;
Drop every little ego-desire
They create pain burning us like fire.

Be happy now
Whatever be your condition;
Unhappiness is the result
Of slavery to the situation.

Be in the present living each moment
Drop expectation of happiness in a future moment;
Do not be a slave of your mental state
If you wish to be free do regularly meditate.

13-6-2001
Almora

BREAK ALL BARRIERS

Break, break my mind
Break all barriers;
Time, space, causation,
These are the barriers.

You are not a slave
Of any thing in Nature;
In fact you are the creator
Of every law of Nature.

13-6-2001
Almora

LOVE ONLY KRISHNA

Love, love my mind
Love only Krishna;
But also know my mind
What you see around is the very same Krishna.

So love all equally
Do every little work joyfully;
Move around cheerfully
Take life's burden happily.

13-6-2001
Almora

LOVE ONLY KRISHNA

Do not concentrate
My mind on the phenomenon of light;
Only in increasing love for Krishna
Dear friend take delight.

Do not concentrate
On yogic power development;
Let truly loving Krishna
Be your sole achievement.

Do not get side-tracked
As you practice your concentration;
To intensify your love for God
Is the sole purpose of meditation.

Be ever watchful
And very very careful;
Every time the motive goes astray
Bring it back do not delay.

14-7-2001
Almora

BE NOT DISTURBED

My mind
Be not disturbed
Be not disturbed.

With
This blank state
Lazy and dull state;
Non-thinking state
Lack of energy state.

Yes
This is surely a handicap
But may be it will help you tap;
All forces spiritual
And conquer forces dual.

So
See this state as a blessing
Drop your bad feeling;
Stop further self-hurting
Know for sure you are growing .

15-6-2001
Almora

HANDICAP HELPS TO SLAY EGO

Yes your handicap do create pain
So what my mind bear a little pain;
Accept it and learn to live with this pain
Look at others and see how much they are in pain.

Compared to theirs yours is really no pain
Do not exaggerate and suffer in vain;
Yours is surely not an unbearable pain
You can be happy in spite of this pain.

By the way dear mind
Who is experiencing this pain?
Isn't it the ego
Through this pain, let it be slain.

You are seeking God
Isn't this true?
How can He come if ego stands
Between Him and you?

15-7-2001
Almora

THE BEST WORK

My mind
You always want to do some good work
You always think of doing some good work;
Your unhappiness is due to your inability to do good work

But may I know what is the definition of your good work?
To realize the Divine in you is the best work
Wholeheartedly devote yourself to just this work;
All your other desires for good social work
Will find it's best fulfillment through this inner work.

So my dear mind
Work, work hard for this one cause
Day and night work hard give no pause;
Love God, love God that is the way.
In His own time in you His glory He will display.

16-7-2001
Almora

WANTING MORE CREATES PAIN

Your handicap my mind
Makes you so unhappy;
It is actually a blessing
Understand and be happy.

You always desired
Name, fame, money and pleasure;
Haven't you got these
Though in a limited measure?

You want more
And that is your pain;
This desire for more
Is a greed useless and vain.

75

Be satisfied with what you have
And stop this craving for more;
Go deep within and seek there
Where lies all –satisfying Divine store.

6.8.2001
Ved Niketan, Swargashram

CONTROL YOUR SPEECH

Control your speech
Control your speech;
My dear mind
Control your speech.

Every time you speak
You pretend to be wise;
This pretension of yours
Is ego in disguise.

You have a need
To feel important
Appear important
Look important

Pretend to be important
Please give up this need.
This is nothing but an act of ego-play
Free yourself from its delusive sway.

21.10.2001
Ved Niketan, Swargashram

SLAY THE EGO

Forget, forget my mind
All your so called pain;
Your handicap and weaknesses
Are meant for spiritual gain.

Chant the Divine Name
With every step you take;
Reminding yourself again and again
I work only for His sake.

You always cry
My mind is not working;
Even if this be true
Isn't it the ego crying?

Slay, slay my mind
Every form the ego takes;
Watch the different ways
A fool of you, your ego makes.

30-10-2001
Ved Niketan, Swargashram

MIND GIVE UP ATTACHMENT

Do not feel bad, do not feel bad
With all the struggles you have had;
You had to work out your own past karma
And now move on in your individual dharma.

When you met you were glad at heart
Let there be no ill-will now that you depart;
Free yourself from all inner pain
Finding fault outside you have nothing to gain.

As we sow so shall we reap
This ancient saying conveys a truth very deep;
Our karmas give us back what we have given before
Acknowledging this truth we grieve no more.

Move on, move on, the God in you
All that you need He will provide you;
Do not harbor hatred, resentment or grief
Your heart will be happy you will find relief.

Giving up attachment try to remain
True soul friend with your love the same.

5-11-2001
Ved Niketan, Swargashram

RENOUNCE ALL DESIRES

Renounce my mind renounce
It is only through renunciation;
To the joys of Divine life
One gets the initiation.

The fulfillment that you seek
Is never found outside;
Those who have found it
Have claimed it to be inside.

Drop dear friend
Drop every little desire;
Roast the seeds of karma
In Divine bon-fire.

9-11-2001
Ved Niketan, Swargashram

PRACTICE HUMILITY

Humility, humility
My friend humility;
In the smallest of your actions
Exhibit extreme humility.

There should be no arrogance
Of any knowledge or wisdom;
Become like a child
To regain your inner kingdom.

Look upon all
With equal vision;
Love all serve all
Do not reason.

Life is a play
The opposites have their say;
Understanding this clearly
From evenness do not sway.

17-2-2002
Ved Niketan, Swargashram

DO NOT REVEAL INNER DIALOGUE

Do not talk
Do not talk;
About this inner dialogue
Please do not talk.

Let this inner dialogue
Be a deep secret in your heart;
By expressing it outside
You tear it's beauty apart.

The message that is conveyed
Is only meant for you;
If you let others know
It will only damage you.

I am always with you
And I love you very much;
To make this love known
Do not crave so much.

18-2-2002
Ved Niketan, Swargashram

EGO HAS TO DIE

Your death is near
You have to die;
Either get killed
Or willingly die.

Drop all protesting
Drop all resisting;
Drop all defending
Drop all fighting.

The world will go on
You are not needed;
The country will progress
You are not needed;
Everything, everywhere will go on
You are not needed.

All your inner decisions
All your inner resolutions;
All your inner conversations
Transform into actions.

I have heard and I realize
Time has come I have to die;
I am ready I offer no resistance
I allow myself to willingly die.

16-11-2001
Ved Niketan, Swargashram

ONE BY ONE DROP YOUR DESIRES

Desires in any form
In the mind it raises a storm;
Creating agitation and mental strife
And a sense of dissatisfaction in life.

It is the ego that is asserting
Through every little desire;
Ruthlessly my mind
Burn them in wisdom's fire.

Let your wisdom fire burn
Intense and strong;
Never succumb to ego demands
And repeat actions wrong.

As the desires in the mind
One by one they drop;
The mind attains a stillness
It's activities come to a stop.

Then the mind becomes
An instrument in Divine hand;
As the Divine flows in it floods
The mind with joy wondrous and grand.

21-11-2001
Ved Niketan, Swargashram

WORK TO MAKE OTHERS HAPPY

You may choose any suitable
Place to stay;
But you have to do
What others say.
Forgetting all your personal needs
You have to work to fulfill other 's needs

By this method you will overcome
Your own ego dictates;
Your present unhappiness in time
Will then lead to a peaceful inner state.

2-12-2001
Indore

DROP THE DESIRE TO IMPRESS

Why, why this desire to impress
And whom are you trying to impress?
What will you get if you can impress
Drop dear friend this desire to impress.

This desire to impress is an ego need
This can create a painful karmic seed
In this world of Maya-illusion
Trying to impress is the biggest delusion.

How long these impressions last?
They are forgotten so very fast.
If you however wish
To permanently impress;
Drop the desire and
Whatever you do will surely impress.

18-4-2002
Ved Niketan, Swargashram

GIVE UP YOUR I

You know I am doing everything
You are to Me like a big boss;
Yet you are so unhappy
To understand this you seem to be at a loss.

Your unhappiness is because
You are not giving up your I;
If you cling to your I so much
Tons of unhappiness you will only buy.

Give up, give up
Your little I;
You know this very well
Your I has to die.

From the burning pyre
Of your dead I;
Will blossom forth the joy
Of My bigger I.

19-4-2002
Ved Niketan, Swargashram

BE HAPPY WITH WHAT YOU HAVE

My mind at last I feel
You have learnt your lessons well;
In your present state of detachment
Please do permanently dwell.

84

No more desiring
No more craving
No more asking
No more begging

Be happy with what you so abundantly have
Do not again crave for what you do not have.

2-5-2002
Ved Niketan, Swargashram

FOR LOVE'S SAKE SEEK GOD

My mind you are seeking Him
For some physical or mental gain;
Seek Him my mind seek Him
But not for removal of pain.

Let your pain remain
Let your problems remain;
Seek Him my mind seek Him
For love's sake seek Him.

21.10.02
Ved Niketan, Swargashram

LISTEN CAREFULLY MY MIND

My mind you have been given
Every form of pleasure;
Stop your incessant demand
For repetition of these pleasure.

You will never again ask
In the tiniest of measure;
I am determined not to succumb
To any form of pleasure.

I have over the years
Gave you what you wanted;
You have on the contrary
Never been contented.

I have now decided
To starve you to death;
Unless you die I cannot
Regain my lost spiritual wealth.

You have been in my life
A very painful thorn;
Casting you aside now
I wish to be spiritually reborn.

I will not give you
Whatever you may want;
I will never again do
What you so much want.

You will now do
What I tell you to do;
You will now go
Where I tell you to go.

20.03.03
Ved Niketan, Swargashram

SEEK GOD ALONE

My mind God alone,
God alone
Day and night seek Him,
Him alone.

While working or eating
Sleeping or dreaming;
Smiling or weeping
Receiving or giving.

Seek Him my mind,
Him alone
Day and night seek Him,
Him alone.

Fill your being with thoughts of God,
Live each moment in remembrance of God.
This world and its charm
Creates only harm;
Know this my mind know this
Seek you therefore your soul's inherent bliss.

8.4.03
Ved Niketan, Swargashram

DO NOT BEG

You torment Me so much
In so many different way;
Instead of coming closer
I feel like running away.

Tell Me dear friend how bored
Were you from a person's nagging;
Do you ever realize how bored
I am from your constant begging.

To use you as My instrument
I have to keep you close;
Do you know what it means to Me
A constant headache in a very heavy dose.

30.4.03
Ved Niketan, Swargashram

BE A GOOD INSTRUMENT

I have made your life
So easy and tension free;
To be able to enjoy this freedom
Drop your ego desires and just learn to be.

To be a good instrument
There is only one way;
Your personal needs and desiring
Has to totally go away.

To be My instrument
Is relatively more easy;
To be one with Me however
Is not so very easy.

As you become a good instrument
My powers and glories I will give you first;
As you learn to handle these
To be one with Me, I will gradually quench that thirst.

30.4.03
Ved Niketan, Swargashram

STOP RESISTING

Whatever demands or requests are made to you
In your day to day life;
Try to fulfill them and do your best
By resisting you create tension and strife.

All forms of resistance
Know this for sure;
Is a product of the ego
Non-resistance is the only worthwhile cure.

Do not resists, do not resists
In this practice deeply persists.

As you practice this
With each passing day;
You will surely see
Your tensions will melt away.

30.4.03
Ved Niketan, Swargashram

DO NOT COMPARE

Do not always compare
With others achievements and wealth;
Appreciate what you yourself have
So much freedom and good physical health.

What you think you have to have
May not necessarily do you good;
Our thoughts and desires are often mistaken
Knowing this change your mood.

Do not grieve for what you do not have
Be happy with what you so abundantly have;
Always remember life is a play
Wealth or poverty both have their say.

30.4.03
Ved Niketan, Swargashram

DROP JUDGMENT

Next time when you talk to someone
Have the feeling you are talking to Me;
Whatever advises or suggestions given to you
Accept them as coming from Me.

The discrimination between good and bad
In the beginning is a genuine spiritual need;
The same process at a later stage
Should be ruthlessly given up and pay no heed.

30.4.03
Ved Niketan, Swargashram

REMOVE YOUR DOUBTING

I can do anything
Learn to totally depend on Me;
Your constant worrying
Is a sign of doubting Me.

If you constantly doubt Me
Then what is My fault?
My grace descending
Comes to a grinding halt.

Doubt is an evil
Remove it from your mind;
Have a childlike faith
Your potentials will surely unwind.

I am always there
To help and protect you;
If you cannot believe this
Then what can I do?

7.5.03
Ved Niketan, Swargashram

REMAIN ATTUNED

Tune yourself with Me
Tune yourself with Me;
Your only task is to
Remain attuned to Me.

Sit quietly with your mind directed towards Me
I will hammer away doubts and worries blow by blow;
Please sit longer each day
Peace and bliss I promise will surely flow.

7.5.03
Ved Niketan, Swargashram

YOU HAVE TO PASS MAYA'S TEST

Why do I always remain
In such an energy less state?
In spite of good food and rest
Why am I always in this state?

How else tell Me do I
Divert your mind towards Me
 If I give you what you want
You will immediately forget Me.

You are very dear to Me
I wish to give you My best;
But for this be very clear
You have to pass My Maya's test.

Give up, give up my dear
All your mental desiring;
Stop your ceaseless grieving, there is
No satisfaction from even fulfilled cravings.

10.5.03
Ved Niketan, Swargashram

LOOSENING MAYA'S HOLD

Name, fame, money and pleasure
These are Maya's tools and treasure;
Renounce my mind ruthlessly renounce these
They are all sources of pain understand please.

To work for your stomach you no longer have a need
Mother Nature will take care, She will feed;
You sit quietly thinking of Me
The trappings of Maya will fall off from thee.

12.5.03
Ved Niketan, Swargashram

DO NOT SHOW IMPATIENCE

I am always with you
Do not doubt this;
I will take care and protect you
From those who try to bite or hiss.

You sit quietly
Your mind absorbed in Me;
Your troubles and turmoil's
Will go and you will be free.

You know this very well
The effort the saints have made in the past;
You also keep making your best efforts
Nothing comes easy or fast.

Nothing is more beneficial
Than My Name please know;
Keep chanting it day and night
Impatience in any form please do not show.

10.6.03
Ved Niketan, Swargashram

REDUCE YOUR SLEEP

Reduce your sleep
My mind reduce your sleep.
Practise more japa
Intensify your tapa

Overcome all laziness
Give up your shyness
Develop more calmness
Give up your sadness

Work hard, work hard
There is no other way;
In your weakness
And your sadness
How long will you
Continue to stay?

5.8.2001
Ved Niketan, Swargashram

PLEASE ONLY ME

I will give you
Many secret information;
As you disseminate them
You will find deep satisfaction.

Do not try to please
Others in any way;
Keep your mind attuned to Me
In every possible way.

I will connect you
To many a disembodied spirit;
As they communicate their wisdom
It will uplift your present low spirit.

You will be given
A very specific mantra;
Which will cure many ailments
And restore a lost science of Tantra.

If people tend to criticize
Or find fault with you;
It is they who will be harmed
Remember not you.

Your honesty and truthfulness
Is much appreciated over here;
Do not feel bad for the discredit
That you get down there.

You will do to this world
Much useful service;
Do not allow your doubting mind
This idea to dismiss.

9.6.03
Ved Niketan, Swargashram

EXERT MORE

Do not lie down
Do not lie down;
My mind please
Do not lie down.

Sit up sit up
Exert, exert;
Ruthlessly drop all desires
For any form of comfort.

The blessed state that you crave
Is achieved through utmost self-effort;
Do not succumb to the tamasic state
Sit up, exert, exert.

18.6.03
Ved Niketan, Swargashram

OBSERVE MOTIVE FOR GOOD ACTIONS

Do not crave for others acceptance
Though it gives a temporary feeling of importance;
It contains within a seed of expectation
And will surely lead to a future frustration.

Do not freely distribute good thoughts and wishes
You may have occasions to regret later;
Observe the motive of your good thoughts and actions
They are generally done for your ego- needs to cater.

Actions done with a motive for praise or recognition
Will surely lead to pain;
If you can do them, do so
But harbor no intention of any personal gain.

20.6.03
Ved Niketan, Swargashram

DO NOT MANIPULATE

My mind please do not be sweet
Loving, caring, compassionate and kind;
To beget praise or some monetary gain
If this be the motive lurking behind.

Drop my mind even the slightest manipulation
In spiritual striving this is a sinful action.
For personal gain if you do manipulate
It will surely come back as hate.

Be honest , truthful and straight forward
In all possible actions and dealings;
If you diligently follow this
You will be free from many disturbed feelings.

In moments of self-defense
Or punishing someone who has done wrong;
Do not twist or torture truth
And make accusations that are grossly wrong.

I have seen this verified
Again and again in my life;
Untruth tends to be stronger in the beginning
But truth always wins in any form of strife.

11.7.03
Ved Niketan, Swargashram

YOU CANNOT HAVE THINGS YOUR WAY

There is a tendency in everybody
To get things done their way;
You my mind drop this desire
To always get things your way.

Things will not happen
However hard you try to have your way;
There is a Divine plan in everything
That will have its own powerful sway.

13.7.03
Ved Niketan, Swargashram

DROP THE DESIRE FOR POWER

Drop the desire for psychic power
Drop the desire for healing power;
Drop the desire for any form of power
Drop my mind these desires this very hour.

Desire for spiritual power is also a ego-need
It is a strong manifestation of lobha, greed;
Take care my mind take care
Do not fall a prey to this side tracking snare.

15.7.03
Ved Niketan, Swargashram

SEEK ONLY ME

Seek Me, seek Me
My friend seek Me;
You are still not wanting Me
You are seeking things and not Me.

Yesterday you clearly saw
A small little expectation;
How it kept the mind for an hour
In a state of deep inner frustration.

Drop this need to impress
By your words or gestures;
This desire in you to impress
My bond of love it fractures.

10.8.03
Ved Niketan, Swargashram

'REPLACE GOD WITH YOUR I'

My friends have told me
To give up my I;
You have told me
My I has to die.

The message is clear
My I has to go;
But how do I do this
May I please know?

Yes, know this to be the way
Use the word God to replace your I;
In every thing you say
Say God instead of I.

Ego in its active state
Is arrogant and showing off is its ritual;
Ego in its passive state
Is defensive and hides behind a garb spiritual.

Shocks and jolts are required in life
To crush the ego-active;
Encouragement and identification with the Divine
Calms the restive ego-passive.

Replacing God with your I
Practice this , practice this;
Your present unhappiness will go
And experience freedom and bliss.

29.11.03
Ved Niketan, Swargashram

ACCUSATIONS AND CONDEMNATIONS

When accusations come
When condemnation comes;
My Lord, My Lord this mantra
My mind you hum.

101

When people overlook your good
And concentrate on your bad;
Repeat my Lord, my Lord
But do not feel sad.

If there is truth in what others say
Then there is nothing for you to feel bad;
If there is untruth they will realize someday
You give up being moody and sad.

12.2 04
Ved Niketan, Swargashram

DO AS I SAY

I want, I want
Drop this wanting;
My Name My Name
Just keep chanting.

What you want
Do you like to do?
Or what I want
You prefer to do?

If you wish to do what you want
Life will be a struggle leading to pain;
If you do what I want
Life will flow peace will be your gain.

Your desiring or My desiring
If they clash;
Headlong into misery
Your life will dash.

So my dear
Attune, attune to Me;
Thru your deep intuitive feelings
I am always speaking to thee.

If you do not listen to what I have to say
With utmost sincerity if you do not obey;
You will find your life, always in a mess
Wanting, craving, desiring but getting less and less.

29.9.04
Ved Niketan, Swargashram

CHANT MY NAME

My Name
My Name;
Just chant
My Name.

Do not look here
Do not look there;
Chant My Name
Just My Name.

Accept your sickness
Accept your weakness;
Chant My Name
Just My Name.

No techniques you need
No practice you require;
Love and devotion to Me
Please carefully acquire.

Right or wrong
Your actions are Mine;
No sin no virtue
Your life is Mine.

29.9.04
Ved Niketan, Swargashram

HOW TO SLAY THE EGO

Watch carefully my dear
In life's every twist and turn;
How the ego re-acts
And makes the heart burn.

Bear patiently My friend
Abuse, insults ,injustice;
Slowly and steadily each day
Put this into honest practice.

This is the easiest way
For you, your ego to slay;
As you slowly master this art
I can then lift you to My heart.

You know this by now so well
I am the good and I am the bad;
Accept calmly My demonic way
Give up mourning and feeling sad.

13.01.05
Marara,Punjab

DO NOT HARM

Know this My dear
You can never have your way;
As long as you intend
Any power or force to display.

The only power I wish you adopt
Love, understanding and genuine charm;
Never even through passing mood
Think of doing anyone any harm.

13.01.05
Marara, Punjab

DROP DESIRE FOR BETTER MENTAL CAPABILITY

Your inability to enjoy your own popularity
Keeps you so much unhappy dear friend;
This desire for better mental capability
Ruthlessly drop it your misery will come to an end.
Desires, desires my mind
They are of many, many a kind;
Each desire fulfilled or otherwise
Leads to a fresh one or tension realize.

The desires of our material existence
We think will give us joy;
No says the wisdom of the sages
In the Self alone abides real permanent joy.

Seek, my mind your own higher Self
That eternal, immortal, blissful Self;
'You are already that', so says the sages
This wisdom has been given to us since ages.

Every desire ties the Soul to physical life
Keeping it in pain, agony and mental strife;
Dropping these desires one by one
The Soul regains its eternal freedom.

5.11.2001
Ved Niketan, Swargashram

LOVE ME

Love Me, dear friend, love Me
With all your heart, do love Me;
We will sing and dance and merrily play
In deep devotional ecstasy, we will sway.

We will convert our love for each other
Into a bouquet of sweet-smelling flower;
To the Lord of our heart, this we will offer
The love that we seek, we find, when He becomes the lover.

26.04.04
Ved Niketan, Swargashram

WHAT YOU HAVE YOU CHOSE

One thing I definitely want
Stop grieving for what you do not have;
Learn to enjoy life with
Whatever you know you have.

What today you do not seem to have
Is because that is what you chose;
Now know you had rightly chosen
This attitude your pain will lessen
I chose and I was not wrong
This attitude will make you feel strong.

13.01.05
Marara, Punjab

LOVE GOD

Love God my mind love God
With all your heart love God;
Call on God with your deepest yearning
Make God your only craving.

Reveal to me my Lord reveal to me
I have no other desire except Thee;
My mind longs my Lord deeply longs
To make my life your creative song.

Bless my life with Thy grace
Reveal to me Thy Godly face;
Away with attachment away with possession
My mind longs my Lord Your attention.

Glory to Thee, glory to Thee
My mind repeat repeat glory to Thee;
In silent moments or in active actions
My mind longs my Lord your attention.

I am Yours my Lord
In body mind and soul;
Thee Thee my Lord
Thou art my only goal.

4.4.05
Ved Niketan, Swargashram

5

MY EXPERIENCES

I AM IN LOVE

I am in love, I am in love
With my own mind I am in love;
My problem was I did not love my mind
Yes to my mind I had been very unkind.
For long have I felt very bad with you
That is why I remained cut off from you.

13-3-2001
Dharamshala

MOON-LIT NIGHT

Ah! this beautiful
Moon-lit night;
What a glorious
Delightful sight.

Tall trees high mountains
Star-studded sky;
Nature's beauty at it's best
I feel so very high.

I tell my mind
This is really grace;
That has brought me
To this wonderful place.

Here surrounded by
Nature's bewitching charm;
I wish my mind awakens
To its own hidden charm.

31-5-2001
Almora

KRISHNA IS EVERYWHERE

Krishna is here
Krishna is there;
In everything you see
Krishna is there.

Where are you then
Looking for Him?
Surrounding you everywhere
It's Him it's Him.

When you smell a flower
It's Him you are smelling;
When you embrace your lover
It's Him you are embracing.

Through every little activity
Through every smiling face;
It is He who is sharing
His infinite love and grace.

31-5-2001
Almora

BLISS IN SIGHT

I was a slave
Of my own thinking;
I was heavily burdened
By own wrong feelings.

I feel now free from all nagging boredom
And am enjoying my newly found freedom;
My heart feels so light so very light
And soul's bliss seems to be in sight.

2-6-2001
Almora

MY SOUL IS AWAKENING

My soul is awakening
From it's long long sleeping;
I feel my joy surging
From deep within my being.

My unhappiness with myself
Was my own big chain;
And this was what for long
Brought me so much pain.

Now I'm free
Freedom gives me peace;
This peace and freedom
Is releasing soul bliss.

4-6-2001
Almora

NATURE NURTURES ALL

Through every little activity
Nature surrounds you;
With so much of Her love
Her presence is for you.

Watch Mother Nature
How lovingly She nurture;
The tiniest of Her creature
Giving each a share of Her treasure.

4-6-2001
Almora

ALL NEEDS ARE FULFILLED IN GOD

What insult, what insult
My mind what insult.

Every time you desire something
Apart from God;
At that moment dear mind
You are insulting God.

What can be of greater need to you than God
What can satisfy the longings of your heart
    better than God?
Yet you keep on desiring everything but God
When will you understand all needs are fulfilled
    only in God.

12-7-2001
Almora

DESIRE TO EARN MONEY

Human love has come
To me at its best;
There is no further craving
My mind is at rest.

The desire to earn money
Is still very strong;
To get rid of this desire
I deeply long

Please Krishna tell me
What is the way?
To free myself from
This desire's disturbing sway.

20.8.2001
Ved Niketan, Swargashram

EGO CAUSES DISTURBANCE

My mind
Every time you get disturbed
Tell me who in you is getting disturbed?
It is the ego that gets disturbed
Let go this ego you will never get disturbed.

My mind
Every time you feel bad
Every time you feel sad
Every time you feel weak and unhappy
Ask yourself who is this who is unhappy?

Tell me my mind
Who is it that feels bad
Who is it that feels sad;
Not you, not you, not the real you
It is the ego, your ego and not you.

20.8.2001
Ved Niketan, Swargashram

MY JUDGMENTS

All those things which once
I thought was so very wrong;
To do the same things today
My mind so deeply longs.

I criticized much and saw in other's
Ego to be very very strong;
Today as I look deep within me
I find my own much more strong.

My judgments of others
Always quick and strong;
It never occurred even once
They may all be wrong.

Today as I look back
I realize I was headstrong;
To give up this bad habit
My mind so deeply longs.

Be calm be tolerant be patient
Do not judge and do not criticize;
That is the way my mind
To be cheerful happy and wise.

5.10.2001
Ved Niketan, Swargashram

EGO IS THE VEIL

Lift Your veil
Oh! Lift Your veil;
From my eyes
Please lift Your veil.

What do I do
Oh! What do I do?
Tell me very clearly
I will do, I will do.

I realize this clearly
Deep in my heart;
It is my ego
That keeps me and You apart.

This struggle deep within
Intense and strong;
Going on for years will continue
How long, how long?

5-11-2001
Ved Niketan, Swargashram

IT'S OK AS YOU ARE

Neither can I sing
Nor can I dance;
Also cannot sit
And get into trance.

Neither can I work
Nor get work done;
Thoughts and ideas
My mind has none.

Okay my mind okay
Relax all this is okay.
I find myself weak
And this is also OK;
I find myself a failure
This too I feel is OK.

Strength and weaknesses
Failure and successes;
Are Nature's opposite forces
Neutralized by evenness.

This is a great lesson
To learn it let me hasten.

9-11-2001
Ved Niketan,Swargashram

SELF- DEFENSE IS EGO PLAY

Self defense in any form
Is a subtle nuance of ego-stuff;
It implies a feeling within
I am not good enough.

Those who judge themselves
As not good enough;
Will invariably judge others
Not good enough.

This judgment of others
And of own self;
Creates tension very strong
And brings hardly any help.

Every time you intend to
Defend any short coming;
At that time you are
Yourself not loving.

Unless you love
And accept yourself fully;
Peace and happiness
You cannot enjoy truly.

28-11-2001
Indore

I WISH I SEEK ONLY YOU

A beast of burden for long was I,
Carrying a load that almost made me die.

Ego, anger and worldly desire
From carrying this burden I wholly retire;
Free and light I quickly move on
With a prayer in my heart for wisdom to dawn.

Wisdom, freedom and love
These I seek is true;
But deep in my heart my Lord
I wish I seek only You.

29-11-2001
Indore

CAN THE NIGHT WISH TO BE THE DAY

This morning again I got up
With a very hollow feeling;
It makes me feel so sad
This frustrating inner feeling.

My mind is always blank
No thoughts come, no ideas come;
With anguish and pain I remain
And a nagging question how to overcome?

Both strength and weakness I understand
Are needed in Maya's play;
So is it right for the night to say
I am unhappy I wish to be the day.

1-1-2002
Ved Niketan, Swargashram

I OFFER MYSELF

I offer myself in Your hand
Like a lump of wet clay;
Do mold me in Your beautiful form
This is what I pray.

Self-effort I have tried
Very little did I gain;
Willingly therefore today
I offer you my life's reign.

5-1-2002
Ved Niketan, Swargashram

I SURRENDER UNCONDITIONALLY

Drop my mind
Even this desire;
To reach a higher state
Do not aspire.

Leave it to God
To decide what He will do;
He knows well
What is best for you.

Surrender, surrender
Unconditionally surrender;
He is doing through you son
What has to be done.

You just sit
And think of Him;
Day and night
Only remember Him.

Rest everything else
Let Him do;
He knows well
What is best for you.

10-1-2002
Ved Niketan, Swargashram

GURU IS COMING

Your Guru will come
In a day or two;
He will guide you
And tell you what to do.

Be very calm
And listen with care;
What you are told
You have to lovingly share.

Your destiny is good
Do not doubt this;
Time has come
You will soon be in bliss.

The joy of Samadhi
You will get to know;
How to get in and out
Your Guru will show.

You will get to know
Who you are;
You will also get to know
How loved you are.

You will get to know
The reason for your birth;
You will get to know
Why you came to planet Earth.

Your so much keen interest
In knowing past and future;
Will now be revealed to you
For you to lovingly nurture.

Your heart will awaken
To its lost glory;
For all the pain you suffered
You will no longer feel sorry.

Love, love, love
This is what you have to share;
Never get involved
In ego's enslaving snare.

You will be protected
From all types of sin;
Go wherever you are wanted
They are all your kith and kin.

7-2-2002
Ved Niketan, Swargashram

I WISH TO KNOW

I wish to know
I wish to know;
Through Your gracious revelation
The secrets of Your creation.

When will you my Lord
Consider me fit;
To receive this wondrous wisdom
From my Guru bit by bit.

You promised to send my Guru
I understood in a day or two;
What happened to that promise
It's more than a month and two.

Please my beloved Lord
Tell me what do I do?
Do I have to still wait
For another year or two?

This waiting and further waiting
To say the least is deeply boring;
I have no choice it is all up to You
Except surrendering what else can I do?

Your game is very painful
Maybe exciting to You;
I neither see nor find any meaning
Spending time wondering what do I do?

12-4-02
Ved Niketan, Swargashram

TEACH ME TO LOVE

The spirit of Radha
Please descend upon me;
The spirit of Meera
Please descend upon me.

The intensity of love
That was in your heart;
May the same intensity
Well up in my heart.

Bless me, bless me
Radha and Meera please bless me;
I wish the Lord to see
And feel His presence in me.

My heart is not yet pure
My longing not yet strong;
Tell me Radha, tell me Meera
What in me, so wrong?

What do I do
To purify my heart;
Teach me Radha, teach me Meera
This sacred, secret art.

1-5-2002
Ved Niketan, Swargashram

I AM WHAT I AM

Even greatness and goodness
I do not aspire;
In wisdom's fire I will
Burn this desire.

All greatness and goodness
I crave in vain;
This craving gives me only
Unnecessary emotional pain.

I am what I am
Satchidananda is what I am
Eternal, immortal, blissful I am
Assert, assert my mind I am, I am.

10-5-2002
Ved Niketan, Swargashram

I FEEL SO HOLLOW

I feel so hollow
I feel so hollow;
In what directions I know not
My actions should follow.

This hollowness, this emptiness
Is eating into me;
When will this come to an end
Please tell me, Oh! Tell me.

Why this hollowness
Why this emptiness
Why this helplessness
Why this unknowingness

Tell me, tell me
Beloved Krishna tell me;
When will You
Fill me, fill me.

27.5.02
Ved Niketan, Swargashram

IS MY EFFORT NOT GOOD ENOUGH?

This pain in my heart
This longing in my heart;
This anguish in my heart
This yearning in my heart.

Is it not good enough?
Is it not good enough?
What is the reason
You do not respond?
What else do I do
To strengthen my bond?

Tell me my Lord
Tell me, tell me;
I wish to know
Please do tell me.

5.9.02
Ved Niketan, Swargashram

I AM NOT LIVING I AM DYING

I am not living
I feel I am dying;
Each day I am passing
Less living more dying.

How long will this continue
My days like this;
I feel so tired
And wish You stop this.

Please at least tell me
How long will this last?
My heart is really breaking
Do something fast.

Come to me my Lord
Please quickly come;
Come to me my Lord
Please, please come.

20.9.02
Ved Niketan, Swargashram

AM I SERVING YOUR PURPOSE

What purpose of Your will
My life is serving;
Will You tell me my Lord
If You deem me deserving.

Am I following Your will
Obstructing or moving in the contrary;
My life feels so empty lacking direction
My mind restless, weak and wary.

What You want of me I wish to know
What I want of myself I do not really know;
I am confused with Your responses from outside
Be so kind enough to answer me from inside.

2.11.02
Ved Niketan, Swargashram

I AM YOUR GURU

You are My instrument
Do as I say;
If you do things your way
From My plans you will stray.

I am your Guru
Do as I say;
You need no more pray
Listen and do as I say.

Stop your restless pacing
Sit still attuning;
Patiently awaiting
My instructions revealing.

I will flood you with My ideas
I will share My power as well;
You sit in attunement with Me
And in ego cravings henceforth do not dwell.

**12.01.03
Ved Niketan, Swargashram**

I AM WITH YOU AS MATAJI

Listen carefully to what I have to say
From the path of celibacy do not ever sway;
Do not touch and do not freely mix
In Me alone your mind you fix.

I will guide you at every step
I will be with you as you take each step;
But be careful not to ever dis-obey
If you do so you will again stray.

Much time you have lost never mind that
As your guiding angel I always sat;
For so many years now do you recognize
The form of Bharti is Me in disguise.

12.01.03
Ved Niketan, Swargashram

I DEDICATE MY LIFE

My life O lord
I fully dedicate;
At Your feet giving up
All personal love or hate.

No more hankering
No more craving;
No more desiring
No more seeking.

I sit awaiting
Your grace descending;
Your joy arising
Your power asserting.

25.01.03
Ved Niketan, Swargashram

DISTINGUISH EGO OR DIVINE GUIDANCE

I will sit
Night and day;
Waiting for Your instructions
And do as You say.

I will be careful
And very very watchful

Not to satisfy my
Own ego needs;
In the pretext of doing
Your guided deeds.

25.01.03
Ved Niketan, Swargashram

I AM YOUR FRIEND

I am your friend
And I am your lover;
My nature's bounty
I will soon shower.

Before I do so
I wish to make sure;
The layers of your mind
Are clean and pure.

Be prepared to give up
Every bit of your I;
As you know very well
Your I has to die.

26.01.03
Ved Niketan, Swargashram

KRISHNA'S ASSURANCE

Today is 'Holi' (Spiritual Festival)
A day of social rejoicing;
For years I have locked myself in my room
My heart heavy and praying.

When will my Lord
My heart be light and gay;
When will I be able to
Sing and dance and play.

You will be given
All powers and glories;
What you have read
So far only in stories.

Wait patiently wait
For the right time;
Your life is destined
To be one sublime.

Certain karmic consequences
Are giving you this pain;
You are however not
Suffering in vain.

As the karmas in due time
Get fully worked out;
You will regain your joy
This do not please doubt.

When exactly this will happen
Cannot be predicted in advance;
The plot of any story
Cannot be revealed in advance.

But for your assurance
Know this for sure;
Your time is near, very near
Patiently a bit more endure.

18 .03.03
Ved Niketan, Swargashram

I AM YOUR GOAL

I am coming to you
Very very soon;
Be prepared to ask
Any desired boon.

Whatever you ask
You will surely get;

Having got what you wanted
You may be trapped in Maya's net.

Be careful as you ask
It is I who am your goal;
It is I alone who can
From all suffering release your soul.

But driven by your mind
If you make a mistake;
For a long time again
You will miss the Divine cake.

8.4.03
Ved Niketan, Swargashram

DOUBT DISBELIEF TOSSING

My mind tossing between
Belief and disbelief;
Waiting for You to come
And give me relief.

This anguish, this deadening
Pain in my heart;
Crushing my sense of well-being
And tearing me apart.

Come my Lord come
And free me from this pain;
Enough have I suffered
Now let Your grace rain.

8.4.03
Ved Niketan, Swargashram

I WILL WASH YOUR DIRT

All promises made by
Me Will surely come true;
Your mind must however
Me alone woo.

I am an omnipotent power
Residing in your heart;
It is the attention of your mind
That keeps you and Me apart.

Focus that attention inward
In total faith and trust;
I will slowly but steadily
Wash away the dirty crust.

10.5.03
Ved Niketan, Swargashram

MAYA IS POWERFUL BUT UN- SATISFYING

Krishna dear Your Maya is really very great
It appears as a well-wisher but in fact is a bait;
To pull those down who are climbing up the tree
For years I was swayed but now I am free.

Krishna dear please do me this favor
Do not side-track me with Your Maya's sweet flavor;
Enough I have had this unsatisfying Maya's pleasure
Open Thou now Your blessed divine treasure.

12.5.03
Ved Niketan, Swargashram

NO SUCCESS IN EARNING MONEY

Name, fame and every form of pleasure
My life has supplied me in good measure;
The desire for money however troubled me a lot
To obtain it many sources I vainly sought.

To earn some money I went to a neighboring town
Didn't get the money the plan got drown ;
Deep in my heart I now fully know
Painful karmic seeds these desires only sow.

Dropping all desiring
And all my restless craving;
My mind lies low
Allowing the inner joy to flow.

12.5.03
Ved Niketan, Swargashram

BEAR PAIN TO WEED THE SEEDS OUT

Pain bearing thoughts
Pain bearing emotions;
Will come up again and again
Creating inner turmoil and strain.

As these emotions come
Know they will again and again come;
Every time they come
O Lord, O Lord, this mantra just hum.

By repeated wrong thinking and feeling
For years we have within seeds growing;
These seeds will one by one surely sprout
By patiently bearing we weed these out.

There is no shorter way
To throw these seeds away;
The only suggestion I wish to convey
'I will overcome' this repeatedly say.

In the fire of intense pain
As we burn day by day;
All karmic dirt's are washed away
And the joy of the soul we gain.

02.05.04
Ved Niketan, Swargashram

DROP RIGID IDEAS

My own ideas about
What is right and what is wrong;
Was very rigid I realize
And unnecessarily headstrong.

Today I wish I fully give up
This faculty that makes all judgment;
And based upon it
All my unnecessary statements.

28.7.03
Ved Niketan, Swargashram

ALLOW FULFILLMENT OF DIVINE PLAN

Observe my mind observe
Calmly, patiently and keenly observe;
But do not act or react take care
Become aware, become aware.

Drop all judgments
And all your pronouncements;
Every action of every person
Has a Divinely intended purpose
Through your enlarged awareness
Allow the fulfillment of that purpose.

29.7.03
Ved Niketan, Swargashram

EGO VS SOUL GIVING

Your ego is persisting
It is still very asserting;
A noble cause it is displaying
I want to help, it is saying.

This desire to help
Is a ego-need has to be given up;
For the spontaneous loving soul-help
In the heart to well up.

The ego does help others outwardly
But strongly craves for a reward inwardly;
The soul helps but craves for no reward
The helping itself, is its sweet reward.

The ego's desire to help
Is by itself not bad;
The soul's spontaneous loving help
However creates no inner reaction sad.

The helper helping through a ego desire
Proclaims himself loud and strong;
A soul giver silently helps
The world's acclaim it doesn't long.

You talk to a ego-giver and see
How much of himself he talks and talks;
You talk to a soul- giver and see
How much he listens, of himself hardly talks.

Ego help does give a sense of satisfaction
But bind's the giver with a golden chain;
This chain even when made of gold
In the long run brings only pain.

As the ego goes out to help
Desire is its motive,
Its end product is pain.
As the soul goes out to help
Love is its motive,
And bliss is its gain.

9. 12. 03
Ved Niketan, Swargashram

LOVING ONE SELF

Do you realize
What makes us wise?
Love my dear love
Wise are those who have learnt to love.

But whom do we love
Are you aware of this?
Your self alone
Never doubt this.

By loving oneself truly
And accepting oneself fully;
We rise to realize the fact
Loving oneself is a sacred Divine act.

So here we go
Away with sorrow,
No thought for the morrow
No beg or borrow,
All pain we burrow
Chirping with the sparrow
The boat of life we gently row.

24.2.04
Ved Niketan, Swargashram

YOUR MESSAGE

Dark clouds in a moon-lit night
What are You conveying, by presenting this sight?
Are You trying to show me
What is happening inside of me.

Your grace descending
My sadness disappearing;
Your love flowing
My heart rejoicing.

Your message is clear
My heart is in cheer;
Your presence I feel, all around me
My life is blossoming, I clearly see.

26.04.04
Ved Niketan, Swargashram

SELF AND MIND

Clear sky, early morning
Soft melodies of birds chirping;
Mind turning inside gently asking
What in life am I seeking?

Why am I vacant and empty
The mind to itself questioning;
Fullness, fullness this is what
In my life I am seeking.

You are full in every way
A voice within persistently say;
I understand in the Self I am full
But how do I make my mind full?

Why the fullness thru mind not expressing
Why the connecting link is missing?
What do I do
To unite this two?

Mind and Self they are one
Why this behavior as if they are two?
The fullness of the Self I sincerely long
To express thru my mind in love and song.

27.04.04
Ved Niketan, Swargashram

REFLECTION AT FIFTY

Still wind, Ganga softly flowing
Descending evening darkness;
My mind quiet, turning in
Desiring stillness.

Life at fifty
Time to reflect;
Draw lessons from the past
A clear direction to the future select.

Mistakes of the past
Not to repeat again;
Sense's slavery and attachment
To be ruthlessly slain.

Do actions based on spiritual wisdom
From egoistic behavior seek freedom;
To the Divine within, ego surrendering
Let actions be done in love overflowing.

27.04.04
Ved Niketan, Swargashram

NO REACTION NEEDED

From time to time life will
In many bad ways provoke;
We should however never
Angry reactions invoke.

Let us sit and watch the mind
As emotions rise and fall;
When the mind attains a peaceful state
We realize, no reactions are needed at all.

Every time we learn to act
Thru this inner calmness;
Pain caused thru emotional judgment
We find becoming less and less

28.04.04
Ved Niketan, Swargashram

I AM MISSING YOU

After a few days
Of very hot weather;
This morning we had
A refreshing rainy shower.

Cool breeze blowing
Fragrant earth smell;
Brings a happy feeling
Divinity in all things dwell.

When life seems hard
And life becomes a burden;
If we remain awake
We see His grace hidden.

In lonely moments
When I feel love missing;
I hear a voice within
Very very comforting.

Speak to Me, speak to Me
I am also missing;
Your love and attention
For ages I am craving.

Through all your pain and suffering
I was gently guiding you;
I wanted you to come back
I was deeply missing you.

Now that you are near
I feel very good;
You will also find
Freedom from mood.

In every difficult moment
You will find Me responding;
In every trial and effort
You will feel My hand helping.

28.04.04
Ved Niketan, Swargashram

DARK AND LIGHT

Clear sky, stars shining
Half-moon slowly rising;
One side dark, the other side light
We are all in a similar plight.

One aspect loving, compassionate, kind
Other aspect angry, depressive, blind;
Two opposite forces within us playing
Keep mind restless inner peace slaying.

How do we reconcile these opposite forces
Where do they come from, what are their sources?
Ego is the cause of all negative forces
Self is the source of all positive forces.

Ego and Self
These two entities;
Their actions and interactions
Creates all complexities.

Ego has to listen and learn to obey
Never allow it to have its own say;
Let Self be the boss and ego its servant
Life will be rich and all things jubilant.

29.04.04
Ved Niketan, Swargashram

MY PLEASANT GAIN

Rain bearing clouds, lightning flashing
Energy is vibrant, powerful and soothing;
Heart is light, no more pain
Mind is calm, no more strain.

Everything easily life is bringing
No more in life clash or struggling;
Years of praying anguish and pain
At last brought me this pleasant gain.
Life is sweet this love I feel
I wish to share, to help others heal.

30.04.04
Ved Niketan, Swargashram

DESIRE SEEDS

Desire seeds of so many kind
Lies buried deep in the sub-conscious mind;
Desire seeds of name and fame
Their power gone, lie low like an animal tame.

Desire seeds of sex alluring
Kept the mind for years fantasizing;
Once in a while with vehemence they rise
Overpowering the mind, creating pleasant surprise.
For most part their impulses subdued
Do not cause any disturbing mood.

147

Desire seeds of uselessness
Helplessness, emptiness and hollowness;
They are as yet indeed very strong
Its grip over the mind I wonder, will last how long?

Desire to be quiet and not seek company
Is increasing day by day;
Talking and mixing appears very boring
Mind seeking within a taste of the Divine Ray.

7.05.04
Ved Niketan, Swargashram

WOMAN SEEKING LOVE AT FIFTY

My life over fifty
My present spiritual needs lofty;
The man I choose my life to lead
Should know me and all my need.

Is he ready to sacrifice
A part of his personal creed;
And be willing to come to my aid
To satisfy my genuine woman need.

Am I in his life a tool
He needs to have his own say;
Or will he be in my life
For my sake, to be with me, my way.

I will patiently await that man who
Loves my womanly presence and womanly charm;
I will never again allow anyone
To use me and then cause me harm.

Men's thoughts and men's ideas I will
Not allow myself to be blown away;
My needs have to be met
From this standpoint, I will never ever sway.

8.05.04
Ved Niketan, Swargashram

TEACHING SYSTEMS

There are trillion mysteries in this world
There are million systems in this world;
Some are involved in creating more systems
Others are struggling to break all systems.

Your destiny is taking you thru all these systems
Your life may need to synthesize these systems;
Each system yells, I am the best
Come to me, I am the fastest, give up the rest.

Go thru all, seek, search and find your way
No beaten track, we have all, to walk our way;
Do not get overwhelmed by the faster, fastest claim
I am original, I am new, I am for this age, they proclaim;

India has seen systems in thousands rise and fall
They appear and disappear like a ping pong ball;
Indian traditions have witnessed and experienced them all
Thru ages the sages in this land gave just one call.

Love, love my dear, love for God
Thru all your seeking you are yearning for God;
Whatever you do just try to see
Love for God should ever increase.

Whatever you do, sing or dance or cook or play
Just do it in His Name, this the sages say;
Thru all the ages, India has stuck to this easy, simple way
I surrender my effort and will, do with me what You may.

18.05.04
Ved Niketan, Swargashram

WHY I FEEL POWERLESS

You always ask why
Your powers have been taken away;
Now know this once for all
You had misused them in everyway.

This life has been given to you
For you to mend your way;
By withdrawing your power I am protecting you
And preventing you going the wrong way.

Your destiny that was foretold
Of which your father felt so nice;
Was over exaggerated in his mind
For which he is paying a heavy price.

Your destiny is however good
And in this later part of your life;
You will reach out to many
And help reduce their inner strife.

Your life is very inactive
This makes you feel so bad;
Your mind is not so productive
This always keeps you sad.

But that was the only way
I could pull you My way;
As you walk your path
Seeking Me and coming My way;
Worldly fame and glory
Will also come your way.

13.01.05
Marara, Punjab

YOUR NAME IS SWEET

Your Name is sweet
So I was told;
Lovingly in my heart
Your Name I hold.

But where is Thy sweetness
That taste I never got;
For so many years now
I sincerely sought;

Will You tell me
My Lord once for all;
When will you respond
To my heart rending call.

21.04.04
Ved Niketan, Swargashram

DESIRE FOR MORE CREATES PAIN

Money, wealth, security
Some say, I need this more;
Name, fame, satisfaction
Some others say, I need this more.

Peace, love, happiness
Yet others say, they need more;
Mental creativity and physical activity
You feel you need more.

My mind this desire for more
Is a pain producing sore;
Drop this desire for more
Since ages, sages have sung this lore.

26.04.04
Ved Niketan, Swargashram

YOU HAVE GIVEN ME LOVE

I have a group of people around me
Each a pure soul a reflection of Thee;
It is such a pleasure to be with them
True love true understanding I always find in them.

Oh Lord! You have flooded me
With so much of Your love;
Will You now not give me
The strength I seek to share this love.

20-3-2001
Ved Niketan, Swargashram

MOTHER GANGA

Mother Ganga much joy to my heart you bring
My soul rejoicing wishes to dance and sing;
Your energetic presence my heart it uplifts
I am grateful to my life to be presented this gift.

Mother Ganga deep in my heart I do aspire
With intense longing and yearning I carry this desire;
May your sublime purity fill my soul
I wish to play your purifying role.

20.8.05
Ved Niketan,Swargashram

6

MY INNER STRUGGLE RESOLVED

My long inner struggle that continued for many years finally came to an end. The struggle is still there but the intensity is very less and creates no pain

I HAVE COME

I have come as promised to you
In your chosen form I will also come to you;
You will regain your confidence day by day
No more will you feel your limitations from this day.

The memory of past lives will be revived for you
Knowledge you have acquired will be reawakened in you;
The hollowness you have felt will no longer be in you
Strength and joy will now bubble up within you;

Your pain and suffering is now all over
Peace and love to many you will now shower;=
Your past was good your future is great
Knowledge and power will now flow down in spate.

Humbly receive and humbly share
I will send you many for you to take care;
Your own will now come back to you
Many a sign to recognize I will show you.

They will come to work for you
The task you have they will help you;
You just sit being tuned to Me
Rest everything will be arranged by Me;

I want your name to spread far and wide
My love for you I no longer wish to hide.

12.01.03
Ved Niketan, Swargashram

MY ROLE IN LIFE

Do not aspire to be a social leader
Your role is to act as consciousness raiser;
Implant strongly value-based ideals
Bring out the best in individual potentials.

As you raise individual consciousness
They in turn will work for social good;
Your role therefore is only to
Nourish them with rich spiritual food.

Your thoughts and ideas towards this end
If you concentrate, My dear friend;
Soul-satisfaction you will then know
And your heart in joy will overflow.

You wanted to be a social leader
My plan was to make you a consciousness raiser;
In this conflict you suffered so long
Having surrendered you will now be strong.

17.04.04
Ved Niketan, Swargashram

FREE OF ALL PAIN

All my pain
I suffered so long;
Were a product of
My ego strong.

As this ego
Slowly dissolving;
All sadness in me
I feel are melting.

Today my heart
Free of all pain;
All vanity and pride
Totally slain.

What else do I
Desire to gain?
An instrument of Thy will
I wish to remain.

29.9.04
Ved Niketan, Swargashram

I AM AT PEACE

Today I can sing
And also I can dance;
I can even sit
And get into trance.

My life has changed
My mind has changed.
Today my heart
Knows no sadness;
And there is no
Sorrow over weakness.

I am at peace
My mind is light;
My heart is enjoying
A soothing delight.

29.9.04
Ved Niketan, Swargashram

SUPER CONSCIOUS STATE

You will surely get
To the super-consciousness state;
You will have to however
For some more time wait.

Let your waiting
Be not be restless;
Develop patience
And practice more calmness.

The higher state you wish to attain
Will not come the way you want it to be;
You will however be in that state
Through your perfect attunement to Me.

17.04.04
Ved Niketan, Swargashram

MY DESTINY IN AMERICA

Yes to America
You will surely go;
They will come and take you
This you may know.

Pleasures of life
You may enjoy in every way;
As long as your attunement
Do not fall away.

Pleasures of life do not bind
If there is no attachment behind;
When 'I' and 'Mine' are dropped from the mind
Pleasures may be enjoyed of every kind.

You have to learn
And teach this well;
Jealousy and possessiveness
Are two doors to hell.

When these are conquered
And mind is free;
The joy of life
You can then really see.

Those who come
To learn from you;
Tell them truthfully
What you are there to do.

You are there
To show them the way;
Renouncing 'I' and 'Mine'
To be happy and gay.

18.04.04
Ved Niketan, Swargashram

MESSAGE FROM THE BIRDS

Three birds, night sky
Flying above my head;
What message dear friends
Have you brought in my aid?

We convey this message
As we pass by;
Your life is beckoning
You have to fly.

To distant lands
As you step down;
Among unknown people
Black, white and brown.

Spread your message
Of love and share;
Many are awaiting
Your loving tender care.

27.04.04
Ved Niketan, Swargashram

WHAT ABOUT MATAJI

She will be here
And you will be there;
She will learn
Your freedom to spare.

Once she will
With you go there;
Thereafter she will
Never interfere.

In her genuine need
Her pains you have to heed;
And come to her aid
When the request is made.

18.04.04
Ved Niketan, Swargashram

7

APPRECIATION TO STUDENTS AND FRIENDS

These are some of my poems written to inspire my students

B'DAY BLESSINGS

On your blessed b'day
My heart longs to convey;
You a pure, pristine soul
Do feel integrated and whole.

Your sincere spiritual seeking
Your dedicated effort and striving;
May flood your inner being
With joy and peace no ceasing.

Let your children grow
And thru their actions glow;
Let your mother's heart in pride
Allow the tears of joy to flow.

May your mind now
Having done its worldly duty;
Seek the Lord of your heart
And His glorious Divine Beauty.

22.05.04
Ved Niketan, Swargashram

B'DAY BLESSINGS

Your B'day happens to be on a very special day
My heart in joy wishes to convey;
May there be many happy returns of this day
May your life blossom the spiritual way.

Your destiny has connected you with a joyous soul
It has given you a loving serviceful role;
May your friendship with Tanya bring joy to you
May it also bring comfort, security and prosperity too.

Your father has achieved much honor and acclaim
May your life also bring you the same;
May you find in life the fullest satisfaction
May love and wisdom shine forth in your every action.

Let us never carry bad feelings for each other
Let us never emotionally judge each other;
Let us always lovingly help each other
Let us in love and respect be always together.

17.6.05
Ved Niketan Dham, Swargashram

MARRIAGE BLESSINGS

Marriage is a union of two souls
To help each other become harmonious and whole;
Marriage is a bond of sacred togetherness
To bless our lives with memorable sweetness.

May you be in your married life
Free from all disharmonies and strife;
May you be a mother and give birth
To bring down souls to enrich this planet Earth.

May you blossom forth as a sweet smelling flower
Through your activities peace and love may you shower;
From Rishikesh I send you my deepest blessings
To grace the occasion on the day of your wedding.

31.8.05
Ved Niketan, Swargashram

VALERIE

Joy to me your company brings
My heart rejoicing wishes to dance and sing;
I wish to love you in such a way
That Divine love is reflected the purest way.

Your presence fills my heart to the deepest core
Never a moment that feels like a sore;
In you I see my Krishna playing
Caring, sharing and sweetly enjoying.

Be bold leave your life in God's hand
In His foundational grace let your life stand;
No doubt, no fear, no despair of any kind
Move on enjoying the present no looking behind.

Life is Light and Darkness in a changing play
Happiness and unhappiness both have their say;
Good moments bad moments come and go
Let us help each other to rise above that flow.

Steamboat
23.8.2011

VALERIE

Our life has been yoked together
For a purpose we do not really know;
Till the divine plan is clearly revealed
Let us in Divine love grow.

Human love even when pure says
If you do this, I cannot be with you;
Divine love on the contrary says
Even if you do this, I will always be with you.

Human love as it transforms itself
Becomes sweeter in so many different ways;
Divine love as it steadies itself
Enjoys life the sweetest way.

Steamboat
23.8.2011

TANYA

Dear Tanya what a joy to be with you
My heart in rapturous waves blesses you;
In this tender age your heart so blessed and pure
God's glory will reveal through you this I am sure.

Practice meditation regularly each night
Concentrate deeply on your forehead light;
Your love for Babaji as you intensify each day
His unceasing blessings will come your way.

Love for God and love for Guru
Let this be the motivation in everything you do;
Arise, awake, realize you are an instrument Divine
Let His love through all your activities shine.

3.4.05
Ved Niketan, Swargashram

ODE TO MICHAEL

Michael you were indeed
A very pure-hearted soul;
You came to Rishikesh very fondly
To strive to attain the life's goal.

Life is eternal
Bodies come and go;
Wherever you are
You are striving for perfection we know.

167

Your shining eyes and smiling face
Your cheerful presence it is this;
For a long time in our hearts
This absence we will miss.

Students come and students go
Few are indeed those who know;
A Divine essence thru us flow
Whose glory their actions show.

Grieving parents and grieving friends
You have left behind;
In the remembrance of your sweet charms
Peace in our heart we find

30.2 04
Ved Niketan, Swargashram

SPIRIT THOU ART, JULIA

My friend you are
Physically quite tall;
You however have a feeling,
You are spiritually very small.

Drop this feeling,
Block the pigeon-hole;
You are so beautiful
Body, mind and soul.

The smile on your face
Reflects what you are;
The twinkle in your eyes
Tell us what you are.

Beautiful, beautiful,
That's what you are;
Joy and love you express so well
That's what you are.

Know this rightly
Truly what you are;
Blessed Spirit, Blessed Spirit,
That's what you are.

13-3-2001
Dharamshala

DIANA

You are a gem
Know this for sure;ʿ
Your heart and mind
Is indeed very pure.

Your hollowness and lonely feelings
Are impressions of experiences from your past;
For months and may be years
Their hold in your mind will last.

Every time these feelings come up
With all the troubles that they bring;
Tell your mind I will not succumb
The glory of my soul I will sing.

I am a soul, I am a soul
Pure and perfect and wholly whole;
Dropping all becoming and its connected pain
The joy of my being I resolve to regain.

24.2 04
Ved Niketan, Swargashram

WELCOME TO INDIA

Come dear Diana to this holy land
And join the sacred seekers band;
Smearing our being with the dust of the soil
Let us unite our might and lovingly toil.

Let us vow to never recoil
From any outer or inner turmoil;
The dark forces let us
Their evil design foil.

Onward ever to taste the sweetness
Let us seek the soul's blissful blessedness.
What can I say more about you
The world will know who truly are you.

Drop all fear
Be very clear;
Your soul is awakening
From its long night dreaming.

No more indulging
In self-pitying;
Know your weaknesses were all a dream
You are an eternal ever-joyous stream.

24.2.04
Ved Niketan, Swargashram

MICHELLE SEEK DIVINE LOVE

Dear Michelle thou art
A beautifully blossoming soul;
Be happy to know your destiny
Is preparing you for an inspiring role.

The loneliness that you feel
The affection that you need;
Are tendencies from the past
In wisdom fire burn these karmic seeds.

We all think human love
Is what we all need;
The sages have all declared
That's an illusion strong indeed.

Drop the craving, drop the desiring
For any form of human love;
Flood the mind with this thought
I seek You my Lord and Your love.

God's love is not an idle seeking
Neither a fantasy nor an escaping;
The soul in this love rejoicing
Fills the heart and mind with joy un-ending.

15.12.04
Ved Niketan, Swargashram

SEEKING YOUR LOVE AND WISDOM

Michelle and Darlene two loving friends
My Lord you so graciously send;
But where are You my Lord hiding
How long will You keep me chiding?

It is Your light and wisdom
That I am seeking;
It is Your joy and power
That I am missing.

When will You my Lord
In this form come to me;
When will I my Lord
In this form enjoy Thee.

Do You my Lord
How painful it is;
This waiting and waiting
That never tend to cease.

Come my Lord come
Deep in my heart I quietly hum;
Your Name, Your Name
My Lord Your Name.

21.04.04
Ved Niketan, Swargashram

MARY

My dear Mary you have a name
In hallowed tradition has much respect and fame;
What stirrings of your soul make you seek me out
Connect yourself within there will be no more doubt.

Ask freely what you have to ask
Do not hold back never keep a mask;
Open yourself up naked as a child
My responses will be warm and mild.

Do you know what you are seeking
Do you know what you are wanting;
The joy of your self
Which you are missing.

Joy, joy and more joy
Our nature is full of joy;
This joy we are seeking outside
But it is found only inside

I will show you the path
And walk with you;
May the Masters in whom you have faith
Bless you, bless you.

21.04.04
Ved Niketan, Swargashram

MICHAL BECOME AWARE

Grace descending
Everybody appreciating;
Life changing
Soul awakening.

Life is treating you really very well
No longer in moods you must now dwell;
Know for sure you are strong and pure
Difficult moments do bravely endure.

Drop all fear
Be very clear;
Many lives you will cheer
Many hearts endear.

Know your unhappy moments are all a dream
You are an eternal ever joyous stream.

11.10.05
Ved Niketan, Swargashram

KRISHNA'S INSTRUCTION FOR SASKIA

Treat her very respectfully
And tell her these words carefully;
Tell her she has very good karma
Let her fearlessly move on in her chosen path of Dharma.

Her heart is filled with virtues and talent
Many a step in spiritual growth she will surely ascend;
She will soon find what she is presently seeking
Tell her to stop all doubting and worrying.

Tell her to use this present now
In strengthening her yearning and learning how to bow;
Many a blessed experience she is destined to receive
Let her be at peace and learn to trust and believe.

6.8.05
Ved Niketan, Swargashram

NADIA

Nadia you have come to Rishikesh
Do you know the reason why?
Upward on the wings of consciousness
You have to now learn to fly.

Honesty, truthfulness, purity
These are the qualities needed;
All your actions, motives, intentions
On these virtues be they wedded.

Exert yourself to mold your personality
To be tolerant, accepting, forgiving, loving;
May your will be tuned to Divine will
And your life blessed with grace unceasing.

6.8.05
Ved Niketan, Swargashram

ANDREA

Through your smiling face and eyes that glow
How to find peace to many you will show;
Presently get involved in removing all karmic weeds
And patiently plant a few useful spiritual seeds.

Go slow in life do not be in a hurry
There is nothing to gain and no loss to worry;
Spend your time enjoying this moment
Past and future let them not torment;

This world is Maya an illusory play
Nothing is permanent nothing ever stays;
Enjoy the moment and sing the Divine Name
Bear all tragedies they are inevitable part of this game.

20.5.06
Ved Niketan, Swargashram

ADI AND LILA FROM ISRAEL

From the Promised Land
Two sister souls;
Came to Ved Niketan Dham
To play their destined roles.

Adi you left behind your fragrance
Thru your lovely B'day painting;
Lila you left behind your sweetness
Thru your gratitude filled singing.

Two beautiful flowers
Blooming in a distant land;
My Krishna I am so grateful
You nourished their souls thru my hands.

26.11.08
Ved Niketan, Swargashram

8

STUDENT'S EXPRESSING GRATITUDE

SWAMIJI

Man of wisdom, strength and high integrity
Compassion reflected through eyes friendly
Consciously choosing Dharma rather than drama
Helping others reducing inner strife
What a beautiful worthwhile life.

With patience, humor, warm heart and deep insight
You sense our needs, intentions, and struggles right
Reaching out to us inspiring and teaching
The holistic path of yoga and cultures blending
A spiritual man stimulating, enriching, uplifting.

Listening to you with open mind and soul
Learning about life and its spiritual goal
Looking at things from a different point of view
Able to discriminate and learn things new
People, religion, culture and more of me
Learning to listen in silence and just being me.

You have enriched my life in so many ways
Deepened my self knowledge and consciousness raise
Intuition instead of impulses, my mind now clear
Patience, tolerance, discipline and no more fear
To put to practice the best possible way
I wish to strive now day after day.

Stefanie (Colombia)

SWAMIJI

To Rishikesh we came from different lands
And fell spell bound in your embracing hands;
Hooked in this Ved Niketan space
Sacred teachings came pouring and so much grace.

Besides this today we all now know
There's a man to whom we can all go;
A story-teller, an actor and who make others sing
A knower of Truth, a teacher and a spiritual king.

Here we came in a moment of confusion
We leave in bliss, no more illusion;
Swamiji thank you and hope to see you soon
If not, may be we will see you on the moon.

**Your's eternal, immortal, bliss- full souls
(Karen, Andrea, Elisabeth, Ganga, Marie)**

SWAMIJI

My thirsty soul a seed with potential
Was hankering for some wisdom special;
A source of water it was earnestly seeking
Nourishment and growth it was deeply longing.

I heard the call of the holy Ganges
I heard the call of the Himalayan sages;
I heard the call of my heart's devotion
Your words Swamiji filled my soul with great passion.

Passion for the love of God
Passion for the joy of life;
Passion for loving service
Passion for dedicated teaching.

The Universe I know today
Brought me to you to stay;
In a mysterious but a perfect way
To express my gratitude I know not what to say.

Your words of truth ring in my mind
Your loving presence compassionate and kind;
A source of joy were you to my heart
It is difficult not to cry as I depart.

Romino, (Chile)

SWAMIJI

Krishna's shining beacon
On foundation rock you stand;
Lost souls of humanity
You bring a guiding hand.

One such soul had washed ashore
Tossed by stormy sea;
Calmness and tranquility
Were your gifts to me.

Heart to heart we shared the ground
The hallowed halls you dwell;
Ananda flowed so freely
As if drinking from the well.

God's grace it brought me to you
By God's grace I shall return;
To kneel before the altar
Krishna's overflowing urn.

Robert (Australia)

SWAMIJI

On the parched garden of my soul
Your rain of wisdom fell gently and sweet;
I had lost the vision of the goal
That's why you and I had to meet

Govinda (Australia)

9

INDIA SHINING

India is shining
And she is gently rising;
She is steadily awakening
From her long deep slumbering.

This slumbering refers to a millennium of foreign domination in which India was reduced to the status of a slave country. Her resources were exploited, her gold plundered and looted, her ancient Vedic education system destroyed and replaced by clerk producing system, her spiritual culture and traditions systematically dismantled and denigrated.

Then the tide changed and numerous enlightened masters manifest in the first half of the 20th century. Men like Swami Vivekananda, who traveled the length and breadth of India, Europe and America, proclaiming the beauty of the ancient Vedic wisdom and the Vedanta philosophy; Shri Ramakrishna Paramahansa and Shri Ramanna Maharshi, whose teachings changed the world; and Mahatma Gandhi, who led the movement for independence.

Her presence in world forums people are feeling
Her strength the world is slowly recognizing;
Her spiritual teachings all over the world flooding
Her philosophy of life the world is accepting.

Her soft-ware engineers the world over booming
Her spirited cricketers, dazzling fireworks displaying;
Her un-friendly neighbor Pakistan painfully realizing
A friendly India better than American diktat bowing.

Her cultural artists are best in the world, this no denying
Her beauty queens ravishing feast laying
　　thru graceful cat- walking;
Her Gods and Deities many home entering
Her Ayurvedic recipes many ailments curing
Her gems and stones body energizing
Her customized 'Yoga' many soul's waking.

Her farmers and laborers, though not yet shining
To compete with the world's best, their hearts are longing.
Her dirty slums and rigid caste-system, though not
　　changing
The Soul of India is radiantly blossoming.

Those who are not aware of India
May I to them strongly assure;
For all the ailments under the sun
Spiritual India has a permanent cure.

Change yourself she declares, before you change others
Reduce your nuclear weapons before you condemn others;
Those who thru globalization exploited the world to the hilt
Have to now thru outsourcing face the coming tilt.

Those who have voiced concern for behavior double-
    standard
Heaven's protection will be with you as a solacing reward.
Economic boom or economic lapse
Both these experiences we have to evenly face;
If fear or despair nags the heart
In this impermanent world this will pass away,
This thought do strongly embrace.

Let us strive to create
A Teresa here and a Gandhi there;
Dropping all selfish concern
Let us learn to lovingly share.

There is only one answer
To all the problems we face;
Manifests your soul qualities
And back to Divinity your footsteps retrace.

Let us assert and strongly resolve:

I will shine forth in joy, peace, love and wisdom.
I will shine forth in sharing, caring and offering.
I will shine forth in honesty, truthfulness and loyalty to my
    principles.
I will shine forth in humility and obedience to what my
    inner feelings tell me.
I will shine forth in loving service and surrendering to the
God in me.

I will shine forth in courage , bravery and fighting injustice
wherever I perceive it.

I will shine forth in stopping those who are cheating and
deceiving people for their selfish ends.

I will shine forth in non-revenge, non-hatred and non
rejection.

Let us pray, let us desire, let us wish and let us act to
manifest the above in both personal and social life.

15.3 04
Ved Niketan, Swargashram

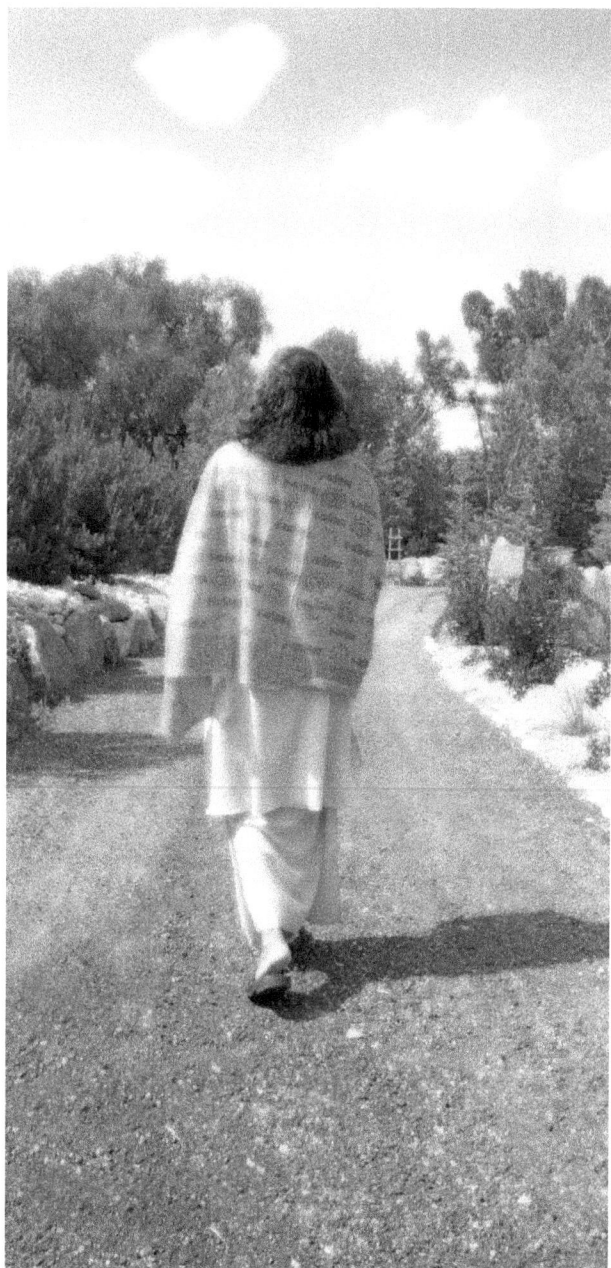

THE AUTHOR

Swami Dharrmananda was born in Kolkata in 1953. Though raised in the Hindu faith, his early years were grounded in Christian Theology; he was educated in a Christian convent.

In deference to his father's wishes, Swamiji was admitted to the prestigious National Defense Academy at age eleven, where he studied the sciences, and became familiar with western psychology and philosophy. He was awarded the Madras Gold medal for sports and graduated from Indian Military Academy as a commissioned officer in 1976.

Though educated in the art of war, a strong inner calling eventually forced Swamiji to relinquish a promising military career. He became enamored with the practice of yoga and took refuge at the feet of his Guru, Shri Vishwaguruji Maharaj in Rishikesh.

He began teaching Yoga and Hindu philosophy in 1985. After many years of practice and study, he was employed as the manager of the Ved Niketan Dham Ashram, where he became Ashram Director in 1988.

Under the guidance and tutelage of H.H. Shri Vishwaguruji Maharaj, he created a thoroughly original training program, an integrated syllabus for the nourishment of the body, mind and soul—combining the sacred essence of Eastern philosophy with the Western sciences in an attempt to elevate the human spirit.

Other books by Swami Dharmananda:

Advanced Yoga Study — A manual for Yoga teachers and students of advanced yoga.

Lectures on the Science of Yoga and Indian Philosophy available on DVD.

To order additional copies of this book and DVD's, please contact:

inneryoga1@gmail.com
sdharmananda@yahoo.co.in

HARI OM TAT SAT
OM SHRI KRISHNARPANAMASTU
OM SHANTI SHANTI SHANTI

www.ingramcontent.com/pod-product-compliance
Lightning Source LLC
Chambersburg PA
CBHW071426090426
42737CB00011B/1579